FATE UNKNOWN

24 Mysterious Missing Person Cases

JENN BAXTER

ISBN: 9798865968382

CASES:
1. Terri Ackerman
2. Yasmin Acree
3. Kathryn Adam
4. Tarasha Benjamin
5. Regina Bos
6. Jodi Brant
7. Leonard Dirickson
8. Lauren Dumolo
9. Jason Ellis
10. Jared Hanna
11. Khiara Henry
12. Anthony Klama
13. Kristi Krebs
14. Steven MacKrell
15. Amos Mortier
16. Lauren Nimbach
17. Patsy Nonemaker
18. Lance Perkins
19. Pepita Redhair
20. Alexis Scott
21. Eric Smith
22. Tonee Turner
23. Christina Whittaker
24. Sydney West

Terri Ackerman

Terri Ackerman was in a good mood when she left her daughter Ambyr's house on the afternoon of Thursday, August 23, 2018. She hugged her daughter and her grandchildren goodbye and told them she would see them in the morning. The 56-year-old then made the 25-minute drive to her house in Lochbuie, Colorado; she called Ambyr around 4:30 pm to let her know that she had arrived home safely.

A couple of hours later, however, Terri called Ambyr back, this time in tears. She was very upset and said that she wouldn't be able to watch Ambyr's children the following day. Terri didn't give any reason for the sudden change but did say that she hadn't slept in a while and was tired. Ambyr told her to get some sleep and not worry about babysitting. She assumed her mother was going to go to bed once she got off the phone with her; she had no idea that she would never talk to her again.

Ambyr worked 12-hour shifts as a 911 dispatcher and was unable to get anyone to cover her shift on Friday, so her fiancé, Jesse, took the day off from work so he could stay at home with their two children. Ambyr's shift started at 3:00 am, so she was up and out of the house before sunrise. Jesse and the children were still half asleep when they were surprised by a knock on the door at 6:00 am. It was Terri's husband, Delbert.

Delbert told Jesse that he had come to watch the kids since Terri was unable to. Jesse was confused;

normally, either Delbert or Terri would have called them ahead of time to let them know about the change in plans. He told Delbert that he had already taken the day off and didn't need any help with the kids. Delbert, however, seemed reluctant to leave. He told Jesse he had already made the drive so he might as well stay there for a while.

Delbert stayed at the house until around 11:00 am, when he left to go to a local marijuana dispensary. He returned an hour later and helped Jesse repair a fence on the property before finally deciding to return home around 1:30 pm.

When Ambyr got home from work that afternoon, Jesse told her about the awkward day he had spent with Delbert. Ambyr agreed that it was odd neither Delbert nor Terri had called them ahead of time to say Delbert was going to watch the kids, but she tried to shrug it off. She didn't think too much of it until Delbert called her that night at 8:00 pm and told her that her mother was missing.

According to Delbert, Terri had been asleep in bed when he left their home that morning shortly after 5:00 am. When he returned that afternoon, he found Terri's wallet, keys, cell phone, and cigarettes on the kitchen counter but there was no sign of Terri. Her car was also left behind. As far as Delbert could tell, the only items that were missing were Terri's prescription medications.

Ambyr was immediately concerned. Delbert told her that he had driven around the area for a while looking for his wife but hadn't been able to find her. He then went to the Lochbuie Police Department and reported her missing at 6:00 pm. Ambyr questioned why he didn't call her until two hours after he had gone to the police station; it seemed odd that he wouldn't have checked with her first to see if she had heard from her mother.

From the first minute she learned her mother was

missing, Ambyr knew that she hadn't left voluntarily. Terri was a devoted mother and grandmother who never would have walked away from her family. She had moved to Colorado with Delbert only a couple of years before and didn't have a large network of friends there. If she was going to go anywhere, she would have gone to Ambyr's house.

Terri had been raised in a strict Southern Baptist home. She suffered from mental health issues from the time she was a teenager, but went years without a diagnosis as she was unfortunately discouraged from seeking psychiatric care. As an adult, she started seeing a therapist and was diagnosed with bipolar disorder; once she was on medication, she became a completely different person. She was much happier and her relationship with her younger sister, Kim, improved greatly. Although they hadn't been particularly close when they were younger, they developed a close friendship as adults.

Terri enlisted in the military when she was 18 years old and served her country for more than ten years. She eventually settled in Maryland and was living there when she met Delbert Ackerman in 2011. After a whirlwind courtship, the two decided to get married. Shortly afterward, they moved to Colorado.

Ambyr, who had a very close relationship with her mother, decided to move to Colorado with her. She stayed with Terri and Delbert for a few months, then she and her fiancé got their own place about 25 minutes away. Terri spent at least three days a week at Ambyr's house, taking care of her two grandchildren. According to Ambyr, her mother lived a very quiet life consisting of "watching her granddaughters, running errands, reading books, and watching the Lifetime channel." She certainly wasn't the type of person who would simply walk away from her life.

When Kim learned that her older sister was missing, she immediately made plans to fly to Colorado, stopping in New Mexico on the way to pick up their mother. She admitted that she had seen a change in Terri after her marriage to Delbert. Kim noted that Delbert seemed to control Terri; although Terri never really talked about it, Kim was upset by how mean Delbert could be and didn't like him.

Things didn't improve any when Delbert's son, Christopher, moved in with the couple six months earlier. He was an awkward man and there was something about him that made Terri uncomfortable.

Family members stated that in the weeks leading up to her disappearance, Terri was secretly making plans to divorce Delbert. She had set up a new bank account and started researching different kinds of state assistance that she might qualify for after she was divorced.

Shortly before she vanished, Terri had told her friend Geraldine that she no longer wanted to be with Delbert. She was extremely upset about the state of her marriage, at times crying hysterically. Geraldine tried her best to comfort Terri and told her that she was welcome to move in with her if she wanted; Geraldine lived alone and said she would welcome the company. This seemed to cheer Terri up somewhat, and Geraldine thought she was seriously considering it. After Terri left her home that day, however, Geraldine never saw her again.

The day after Terri was last seen, Ambyr decided to pay Delbert a visit. She didn't call to let him know she was coming, and when she got there she found Delbert and Christopher deep in conversation. When they realized Ambyr was there, they immediately stopped talking. Christopher walked towards the back of the house while Delbert greeted Ambyr.

Ambyr noted that Delbert's white pickup truck, which was usually parked in the driveway, was missing. Oddly, all the trash cans and recycling bins were also empty, despite the fact that there had been no trash pickup that day. Inside, her mother's normally overflowing ashtray had only one cigarette butt in it.

Police searched the home and the surrounding area but found nothing to indicate that foul play had taken place. After Ambyr pointed out that Delbert's truck was missing, an officer asked him where it was. He said that it was at his son's shop for bodywork; it had a number of dents that needed to be fixed. The officer accepted this explanation. A few days later, however, the truck was back at the home, complete with all of its dents. No bodywork had been done. It's unclear if investigators followed up on this discrepancy.

Terri's family distributed missing person flyers throughout the area and begged for anyone who had seen Terri to contact police. Although they wanted to believe that Terri was still alive and would be found safe, as days went by without any word from her, their optimism started to fade.

A search and rescue team used trained dogs to comb through the area surrounding Terri's home but were unable to find any clues pointing to Terri's whereabouts. Bloodhounds were able to pick up her scent at her home but were unable to follow it off the property.

Three months later, Terri was still missing and Ambyr admitted that she feared the worst. The family had managed to get through Thanksgiving without her, but they were dreading the upcoming holiday season. Ambyr told a reporter, "I just really, really want someone to come forward and let us know something...something isn't right."

Ambyr worried that her mother's case wasn't getting the attention it deserved, either from police or the local media. She noted that it had been overshadowed by the murders of Shanann Watts and her two young daughters, which had occurred less than two weeks before Terri went missing. The case had attracted the attention of both the local and national news media; Terri's case received only a small fraction of the publicity.

Lochbuie Police Chief Tracey McCoy noted that investigators had been collaborating with agents from the Colorado State Bureau of Investigation and detectives from the Weld County Sheriff's Office since the start of the investigation, but they had exhausted all leads and still didn't know what had happened to Terri.

Ambyr insisted that her mother never would have disappeared voluntarily; she was convinced that foul play was involved. "She was happy…her family was everything…she just wouldn't do this to us." Chief McCoy admitted that foul play hadn't been ruled out, but detectives had no solid evidence to suggest that it had occurred.

It was clear that the family believed either Delbert or his son had something to do with Terri's disappearance. Delbert admitted to Kim that he and Terri had argued the night before she went missing; he claimed that he had been trying to explain how to use their new microwave to her but she didn't seem to understand. Kim thought Delbert sounded angry over the incident; the family couldn't help but wonder if their verbal altercation had escalated into physical violence.

Investigators asked Delbert to take a polygraph examination about Terri's disappearance and he agreed to do so. Although the results of the test were not made public, police have never publicly named him as a suspect.

Christopher was also asked to take a polygraph but he refused. He told Ambyr that he had absolutely no idea what had happened to her mother and saw no reason to take a lie detector test.

Chief McCoy admits that Terri's disappearance is concerning, especially as it has now been more than five years since she was last seen, but has stressed that there is no evidence to support the theory that foul play was involved. He has also stated that there is no evidence pointing to any potential suspects.

Terri's family has been very open about the fact that they believe Terri met with foul play and was likely murdered hours before she was reported missing. They refuse to give up their search for answers and remain hopeful that someone will come forward with the answers they need to finally bring Terri home.

Terri Ackerman was 56 years old when she went missing in 2018. She was a devoted mother and grandmother who is deeply missed by her family; they don't believe she went missing voluntarily and are convinced that she was a victim of foul play. Terri has hazel eyes and red hair, and at the time of her disappearance, she was 5 feet 4 inches tall and weighed 170 pounds. She has a full sleeve tattoo of fairies and leaves on her right arm, and tattoos of baby footprints on the side of her chest, a fairy on her back, a band with feathers on her upper left arm, and one of a baby with wings on her lower left arm. She also has tattoos on each calf. If you have any information about Terri, please contact the Lochbuie Police Department at 303-659-1395.

Yasmin Acree

Yasmin Acree hadn't had an easy life. The 15-year-old's mother had lost custody of her and her brother when they were toddlers; they were part of the Kentucky foster care system until 2001, when they were placed with Rose Starnes in Chicago, Illinois. Rose was their aunt by marriage, and she formally adopted the siblings in 2006. In 2007, however, Yasmin's 16-year-old brother moved out of her home.

On the evening of Tuesday, January 15, 2008, Rose and her daughter decided to spend the night at a casino in Elgin, Illinois. Rose's live-in boyfriend remained at home with Yasmin. The teenager had spent the afternoon at the North Lawndale YMCA and was tired when she got home, but wanted to do a load of laundry before she went to bed. After finishing her laundry, she headed to her small bedroom in the basement of the home. The following morning, she was gone.

When Rose's boyfriend woke up Wednesday morning, he noticed that Yasmin wasn't home but assumed that she had already left for school. He didn't mention anything to Rose when she got home that afternoon; it wasn't until Yasmin didn't come home at her normal time after school that Rose realized there was a problem.

When Rose checked Yasmin's bedroom, she noticed that the door leading to her basement room from an alley behind the house appeared to have been forced open. A gate leading to the home, which was usually kept padlocked, was also open. Rose discovered that the padlock had been cut off. She immediately called the Chicago Police Department and said that her daughter had been abducted.

Despite the fact that a padlock had been cut, police told Rose that they didn't see any signs of forced entry. In their minds, Yasmin had simply run away from home and would return when she felt like it. This was confirmed when several of her friends from school claimed that Yasmin had told them she had been thinking about running away. Although police entered her name into a missing person database, they didn't launch any kind of search for her.

Rose was certain that Yasmin hadn't run away from home. Although the teenager struggled with some emotional and behavioral issues stemming from abuse she had suffered as a child, she was maturing into an intelligent young woman and had no history of running away. She was an excellent student who had won a regional spelling bee the previous year; she had also been the salutatorian of her eighth-grade class at May Elementary Community Academy.

At the time of her disappearance, Yasmin was a freshman at Austin Polytechnical Academy in Chicago. She was a popular student who loved to talk, sometimes too much. Teachers laughingly recalled how they would often have to urge her to stop talking in the hallways so she could make it to her next class on time.

Yasmin enjoyed spending much of her free time at the YMCA, where she participated in a number of different sports. She had been thrilled when she had been selected to enter their mentoring program and had been looking forward to attending one of their retreats that summer.

Kimberly George, the director of the youth and teen development program at the YMCA, told reporters that Yasmin was smart and sociable; she was always very attentive to the needs of younger members and officials had been considering her for a position in a new summer job program. Like Rose, Kimberly did not believe that Yasmin would have run away from home.

Rose was convinced that police had dismissed Yasmin as a runaway solely because of her race, although age likely played a role in their decision as well. She couldn't believe that they hadn't conducted any sort of investigation at the home, especially since it was clear that the lock on the gate had been cut. She enlisted the help of several prominent religious leaders in the city; the resulting publicity forced police to take another look at the case.

Two days after Yasmin vanished, investigators returned to the home. This time, they collected the lock that had been cut from the gate as evidence; it was analyzed for fingerprints but none were found. Officials with the Chicago Police Department would later admit that it had been a mistake to not process the scene when Yasmin was first reported missing, though they didn't believe it had too much of an impact on the later investigation.

Months went by with no progress on the case. In July, Rose, flanked by family, friends, and several ministers, gathered in front of the Chicago Police Department headquarters to protest what they believed had been a lackadaisical investigation. Rev. Marshall Hatch, the pastor of a local Baptist church, told reporters, "Because she's a 15-year-old African-American from the West Side, this case isn't getting the attention it deserves."

Chicago Police Cmdr. Joseph Salemme said that the

criticism was insulting. He pointed out that detectives had spent more than 2,000 hours working on Yasmin's case, following leads in both Illinois and Kentucky. They had sent several pieces of potential evidence to the state crime lab for analysis, but had been unable to develop any suspects in the disappearance. Officials also noted that not everyone associated with the missing teenager had been cooperative in the investigation.

Yasmin should have celebrated her 16th birthday on October 25, 2008, a milestone she had been looking forward to. Instead of hosting a sweet 16 party, Rose was still working to keep Yasmin's name in the public eye. It was an uphill battle; the local news media paid scant attention to the missing teen's case.

Another year passed and Yasmin was still missing without a trace. There had been a few scattered sightings of her reported, but none of them could be confirmed and those who knew her were certain she would have contacted one of them if she were able. Rose still hoped that she was alive and would return home. She left Yasmin's tiny bedroom in the exact condition it had been on the day she was last seen, with her clothing neatly folded in her dresser and her bed covered in stuffed animals.

Rose was still confident that Yasmin hadn't run away from home, but admitted that things hadn't always been great between her and her adopted daughter. She sometimes had trouble dealing with Yasmin's behavioral issues; there had been times when she got so frustrated that she had whipped Yasmin with a belt and locked her in the basement. She also admitted that she had kicked Yasmin's brother shortly before Yasmin went missing, something that likely upset the teen deeply.

Yasmin had managed to hide whatever problems

she had at home; her classmates and those who knew her from the YMCA had been unaware of the issues she had with Rose. Still, they didn't think the teenager would have left on her own; although intelligent, she had a childlike side and wasn't the type to wander off alone.

In 2011, the National Center for Missing and Exploited Children released an age-progression photo of Yasmin. The resulting publicity helped revive her case and investigative reporters for the Chicago Tribune decided to take a deeper look at the circumstances surrounding her disappearance.

Rose sat down with the reporters and allowed them to have access to Yasmin's room. While looking through her things, one of the reporters found something that had the potential to be a key piece of evidence: Yasmin's diary. They were disturbed by what they found. According to the Tribune's editor, Gerould Kern, "Our reporters encountered information that suggests a serious crime may have been committed." They went directly to the Chicago Police Department and reported their findings.

The last entry in Yasmin's diary had been written just a few weeks before she vanished, providing police with an intimate look into what was going on in her life in the weeks and months leading up to her disappearance. There were two references to a man named Jimmie Terrell Smith, a 35-year-old ex-convict who had rented the upstairs apartment in Rose's Two-Flat home.

Jimmie had moved into Rose's building shortly after he had been released from prison; he had served more than 10 years after being convicted of attempted murder. Although he moved out by the time Yasmin disappeared, according to friends he had continued to contact her. By the time police learned this, Jimmie was back in jail charged with raping five women – two of whom were just 14 years old.

Jimmie agreed to speak with reporters from the Chicago Tribune while he was in jail awaiting trial. He claimed to have no involvement in Yasmin's disappearance but admitted that he did know what had happened to her. He wouldn't give any details but seemed to indicate that she was no longer alive.

During the initial stages of the investigation, Rose never mentioned anything about Jimmie to police; they didn't learn he had rented an apartment from Rose until more than a year after Yasmin went missing and they had been unaware that he had any interaction with the missing teenager. Although Rose later claimed she had suspected from the start that Jimmie might have been involved in Yasmin's disappearance, she said she didn't mention it to police because she had no evidence and didn't want to hurt his reputation.

Detectives interviewed Jimmie on several occasions in 2011, hoping he would break down and tell them where Yasmin was. At one point, they obtained a search warrant for a house belonging to one of Jimmie's ex-girlfriends but failed to find anything relevant to their case. Although no evidence has been found linking him to Yasmin's case, he remains a person of interest.

Yasmin Acree was just 15 years old when she went missing in 2008. She was a sweet and intelligent teenager who had been failed by many people in her life, starting with her own mother. Although police originally considered Yasmin a runaway, they now admit that foul play was likely involved in her disappearance. Yasmin has brown eyes and brown hair, and at the time of her disappearance, she was 5 feet 2 inches tall and weighed 125 pounds. *She was last seen wearing pajamas; it is unclear if any other items of clothing were missing from her home. If you have any information about Yasmin, please contact the Chicago Police Department at 312-746-8365.*

Kathryn Adam

Kathryn Adam left her Salina, Kansas, home before dawn on the morning of Wednesday, April 29, 1993. The 35-year-old drove her L'eggs company van to a local Kwik Shop, where she bought gas, a newspaper, and a cup of coffee. She then headed for Triplett's Mini Storage, located at the corner of Magnolia and Centennial Roads, where she started to load the Ford Econoline van with the L'eggs products she needed to complete that day's deliveries. She never made any deliveries that day; she was never seen again.

Kathryn's 16-year-old daughter, Laura, was not too concerned when her mother wasn't at their apartment when she got home from school that afternoon. Although it was unusual for her to come home to an empty apartment, she thought maybe her mother had gotten caught up at work or had met up with a friend on the way home. As hours went by, however, she started to worry that something might be wrong.

Since Kathryn didn't work out of an office, Laura had no way of getting a hold of her while she was at work. As she waited anxiously for any word from her mother, she eventually fell asleep. She woke up early Friday morning with the feeling that something was wrong and immediately searched the small apartment for any sign of her mom. It was clear that Kathryn had never returned home the previous night.

Laura started calling some of her mother's coworkers and learned that Kathryn hadn't made any of her scheduled store visits on Thursday. When Laura got off the phone, she knew that something was wrong. She called the Salina Police Department and reported her mother missing.

Laura told police that she had last seen her mother around 11:00 pm on Wednesday, right before she went to bed. When she woke up for school on Thursday, her mother had already left the apartment to go to work. Investigators immediately issued a BOLO for both Kathryn and her white work van.

After speaking with Kathryn's boss, investigators learned that Kathryn kept her L'eggs inventory at Triplett's Mini Storage, about three miles away from her apartment. She would go there each morning to pick up the products she needed to restock at various retail stores that day. Detectives were sent to the storage facility to see if they could find any clues to Kathryn's whereabouts.

As soon as investigators arrived at Kathryn's storage unit, they knew that they weren't dealing with a routine missing person case. The door to the storage unit was open and there was a small amount of blood inside. There was more blood in the parking lot right outside of the unit, as well as a few items of L'eggs merchandise. Detectives theorized that Kathryn had been in the process of loading her van with products when someone attacked her.

Around 6:00 pm, investigators learned that Kathryn's van had been found just two miles away from the storage unit. It had been abandoned in the parking lot of Russell's Restaurant, which was closed at the time for renovations. The van was muddy and appeared to have been driven off-road recently. When they looked inside, they found that the back of the van was covered in blood.

There was no sign of Kathryn.

Investigators assumed that the blood found in the storage unit and van belonged to Kathryn but weren't sure if she had been killed. It was possible that she was injured but still alive, so they appealed to the public for help in locating her. They also wanted to hear from anyone who had seen either Kathryn or her van on Thursday or Friday.

After reading about the disappearance in a local newspaper, the overnight clerk at the Kwik Shop on Crawford Street called police and told them that he had waited on Kathryn Thursday morning. She had stopped to fill up her gas tank before heading to the storage unit to pick up her merchandise; while there, she had picked up a newspaper and a cup of coffee. The store had surveillance cameras, which showed Kathryn leaving the store, alone, at 4:33 am. If someone had followed her from the gas station to the storage facility, they were not captured on surveillance footage.

Kathryn kept meticulous mileage records in her van, so investigators were able to tell exactly how many miles the van had been driven since she filled up the tank Thursday morning. Although police have never confirmed the distance the van had been driven, it was rumored to be 60 miles. This would mean Kathryn could have been taken anywhere in a 30-mile radius of Salina. It was a vast area to search.

Police started driving through the rural area, searching along culverts and in isolated fields. They looked for any signs of trampled grass that could indicate the van had been driven there but came up empty. Their search was hampered by the fact that heavy rain moved into the area, erasing potential tracks.

After receiving a tip from a woman who thought she saw a white van parked by the intersection of Burma and Magnolia Streets, investigators searched through a one-mile section of land near there. They found nothing.

The Kansas State Police used their helicopter to fly over Saline County with a thermal imaging camera in an attempt to locate Kathryn or her body. They flagged several locations where they thought they might have seen something, but when investigators checked each one out they didn't find anything relevant to their investigation.

While the physical search for Kathryn was underway, detectives began interviewing everyone who knew her in hopes of finding some clue as to what had happened to her. They started with her immediate family.

Kathryn was the oldest of two daughters born to Harry and Mary Swendson in Atchison, Kansas. She was a bright child; during her time at Effingham Junior High School, she was consistently on the honor roll. She loved music and was a member of her school's band and chorus; she also sang in her church choir.

She went to Atchison High School and maintained excellent grades during her freshman and sophomore years, but soon fell in with what her mother called "the wrong crowd" and started using drugs. Her grades declined and her parents decided they didn't want to deal with her behavior so she was sent into foster care.

Kathryn's foster family lived in Hope, Kansas, and she started her junior year at Hope High School. It was there that she met and fell in love with Gerald Adam; the feeling was mutual and they got married in the fall of 1975 when Kathryn was only 17 years old. After the wedding, Kathryn still managed to complete high school, graduating from Topeka High School in 1976.

Gerald and Kathryn eventually moved onto a farm in Solomon, Kansas. Kathryn worked various odd jobs while Gerald worked on the farm and as a truck driver. Two years after they got married, their only child, Laura, was born. Although those who knew the couple believed they had a great relationship, Laura would later say that it was not a happy home. According to her, neither Kathryn nor Gerald had really wanted to be parents and they didn't seem to get along very well.

Laura stated that her mother was a very involved parent who attended all of her sports games when she was in school and enjoyed cheering her on. Laura didn't have a great relationship with her father, who spent most of his time on the road as a truck driver and would simply ignore Laura when he was home.

In early 1993, Kathryn apparently decided that she had enough of Gerald. She had two deputies accompany her to the family farm one afternoon and stand watch while she gathered some of her and Laura's belongings. Kathryn and Laura then left the home, never to return.

In March 1993, Kathryn rented a one-bedroom unit at the Iron Crest Apartments in Salina. Although it meant that she and Laura were pressed for space, it was only temporary; she planned to upgrade to a two-bedroom in a couple of months. She got a job with the L'eggs Hosiery Corporation shortly after moving into the apartment.

Kathryn had some reservations about her new job; she didn't like the fact that she had to leave the apartment while it was still dark and go to the storage unit alone. Still, the early hours allowed her to have her afternoons free, and she wanted to be home when Laura returned from school each afternoon. She soon settled into a routine and everything went well until the morning of April 29th.

Kathryn had been tired when she got up for work that Thursday morning; she attended a play at the Salina Community Theater with friends the night before and had been late getting home. It was nearly 11:00 pm by the time she returned to her apartment, giving her just a few minutes to chat with her daughter before both of them headed to bed. She was up and on her way to the gas station by 4:20 am.

Everything appeared to be normal when she stopped by the Kwik Shop; she chatted briefly with the clerk while paying for her purchases and walked out the door with a newspaper in one hand and a cup of coffee in the other. Detectives assumed that she then left the gas station and went straight to the storage facility to start loading up her van. She likely hadn't had time to enjoy more than a few sips of her coffee before she was attacked.

Investigators were unable to find anyone who might have wanted Kathryn killed. Her estranged husband was interviewed extensively but detectives were unable to connect him to the crime. Although Laura would later tell reporters that her parents had a troubled relationship, Kathryn's mother had nothing but praise for Gerald, calling him the nicest, kindest man she had ever known.

Kathryn hadn't lived in Salina long enough to make many close friends, but she had bonded with Maxine Rogers, the manager of the Iron Crest Apartments. Like Kathryn, Maxine was the mother of a teenage daughter; she told police that Kathryn's life revolved around Laura and they seemed to have a very close mother-daughter relationship. Maxine was aware that Kathryn was in the process of getting a divorce, but said she never spoke ill of her estranged husband and didn't appear to be afraid of anyone.

Due to the nature of her job, Kathryn hadn't had a chance to get to know many of her co-workers well. She spent her days alone, driving her L'eggs van to different retail stores to restock their hosiery section and let management know of any upcoming sales and promotions. Her visits usually only lasted 15 to 20 minutes; store employees told police that she was always polite and professional but didn't share any personal information with them.

Despite their intensive investigation, detectives were unable to find any clue to Kathryn's whereabouts. Her family continued to pray for a miracle but officials admitted that they believed Kathryn was dead. They assumed that her white van had been used to dispose of her body and they made several public appeals for information, hoping someone might have seen the van Thursday morning. They followed up on each tip they received but none of them led to Kathryn's body.

Within a couple of weeks, tips started to dwindle and the case slowly went cold. Investigators noted that the sheer size of their county – and the large number of isolated spaces where a body could potentially be dumped – made it nearly impossible for them to fully cover the entire area.

For Kathryn's family, the wait was excruciating. Laura was put into foster care after her mother's disappearance; at a later hearing, she told the judge that she didn't want to live with her father. Gerald, who refused to even glance at his daughter during the hearing, told the court that he was unable to take care of her and his parental rights were severed. Laura would never see him again.

Kathryn's parents tried to hold onto the hope that she was still alive somewhere but knew that she never would have abandoned her daughter. Mary admitted that she and Kathryn had gone through a rough period when Kathryn was a teenager but had settled their differences in later years and had a close relationship. She and her husband offered a $1,000 reward for information leading to Kathryn's recovery, but it failed to bring in any new leads.

Months and then years went by, and the mystery of what happened to Kathryn remained unsolved. Both the Salina Police Department and the Kansas Bureau of Investigation continued to investigate her disappearance but had exhausted all leads and didn't believe the case would be solved unless someone came forward with the information they needed to finally locate Kathryn.

In June 2001, Kathryn's case was featured on billboards in Saline County; investigators hoped that this would remind the public that she was still missing and bring in some fresh leads. Although a few tips were called in, no substantial developments were made. Her case faded from the headlines and once again went cold.

Although Kathryn's body has never been located, detectives believe she was murdered and her case had been classified as a homicide. There have been no new developments in years but investigators still hope someone will come forward with the information they need to finally determine what happened to Kathryn on that cold April morning.

Kathryn Adam was 35 years old when she went missing in 1993. She was just starting a new chapter of her life at the time; with a new job and a new apartment, things were looking bright for her and her daughter. Kathryn has brown eyes and brown hair, and at the time of her disappearance, she was 5 feet 4 inches tall and weighed 120 pounds. She was last seen wearing dark-colored pants, a light-colored blouse, and a Kansas City Royals jacket. Due to the circumstances surrounding her disappearance, detectives believe Kathryn met with foul play. If you have any information about Kathryn, please contact the Salina Police Department at 785-826-7210.

Tarasha Benjamin

Tarasha Benjamin loved going to the Selma Flea Market in her hometown of Selma, Alabama. The 17-year-old would normally go to the flea market every Saturday, and June 26, 2010, was no exception. Tarasha told her mother, Regina Benjamin, that she and a family friend, Telish Givhan, were going to go to the flea market together that morning; they left the house around 9:00 am. It was the last time Regina would see her daughter.

Telish returned to the Benjamin home around 1:00 pm without Tarasha; she told Regina that something had come up and she had decided not to go to the flea market; she said she let Tarasha borrow her truck so she could drive herself there. She assumed she would be back by then and had come to retrieve her vehicle.

Regina immediately tried calling Tarasha's cell phone but it went straight to voicemail. Concerned, she started calling friends and other relatives who lived in the area to see if any of them had seen her daughter. Theresa Pugh, a family friend, told Regina that she had seen Tarasha driving in the neighborhood around 10:30 am. "I saw her go around the corner. She was driving [Telish's] truck...she was by herself."

One of Regina's cousins told her that she had seen the gray Mazda truck Tarasha had been driving parked on Cecil Jackson Boulevard near an American Apparel store. Regina and other family members went looking for the truck and found it parked exactly where the witness had seen it. Ominously, two of the windows on the driver's side had been broken, as had the handle on the driver's door. There was no sign of Tarasha.

Regina called the Selma Police Department and reported her daughter missing. She told them that Tarasha was the type of teenager who would check in several times a day when she was out; it was completely out of character for her to go anywhere without letting her mother know where she was going to be. Regina was convinced that something terrible had happened to her.

By Sunday, Tarasha's family members and friends had launched an extensive search for the missing teenager. They canvassed the city of Selma, distributing missing person flyers and interviewing residents looking for anyone who might have seen Tarasha after she left to go to the flea market.

One witness claimed he saw Tarasha and two other girls walking along Union Street near the Bosco Center late Saturday night; the two girls kept walking down an alley but Tarasha stopped when she saw a black Dodge Charger pull up to the curb. It's unclear if the man saw Tarasha or just someone who looked like her. According to Regina, "He said she got into that black Charger...I don't know, I just don't know." Tarasha wasn't the type of person who would get into a car with a stranger.

On Monday, Tarasha's loved ones met at the Selma Police Department and spoke with detectives about the teenager's disappearance. After the meeting, they spread out across the city to search for Tarasha. Angela Benjamin, Tarasha's cousin, was a Selma city councilwoman. She took the lead in the search effort, sending volunteers to different sections of the city to look for Tarasha. She also started a Facebook page dedicated to finding Tarasha and pleaded with people to contact them if they knew anything about what had happened to Tarasha. "We just need information. Every lead is being followed up, every last one."

As loved ones started canvassing the city, they were interrupted by the sound of sirens. A call had come in about a potential altercation involving Tarasha, and several police cars sped across the Edward Pettus Bridge to follow up on the report. The call had come in from a man named Wesley Bell, who had been driving home from work when he spotted a man he knew as Charles walking along the side of the road. Thinking he might need a ride, Wesley pulled over alongside Charles.

Wesley's sudden appearance seemed to spook Charles. "Before I could talk to him, he said, 'I ain't done nothing' and ran away." Confused, Wesley chased after him as he ran off into a wooded area next to the road. He asked why he was running if he hadn't done anything but got no response from Charles. He lost sight of Charles but saw that he had dropped a bloody towel. He picked it up, telling police that "it looked like evidence." It's unclear why Wesley assumed that Charles and the bloody towel had anything to do with Tarasha's disappearance; investigators and volunteers spent the rest of the day searching the area for Charles but were unable to locate him and he was never linked to Tarasha.

In another twist, Telish Givhan was arrested that Monday on an outstanding warrant and was being held in Dallas County Jail. Although Selma Police Detective Sgt. Tory Neely stated that her arrest had nothing to do with Tarasha's missing person case, the timing was suspicious and some wondered if she knew more than she was saying about the disappearance.

By Wednesday, Tarasha's loved ones were growing increasingly desperate to locate her. That afternoon, a group of family, friends, and volunteers met at a performing arts center in Selma to discuss the search effort. Selma Mayor George Evans addressed the group, admitting, "This is a real sad occasion. People come up and get lost, that's what I hope this is." Those who knew Tarasha, however, were certain that she wasn't simply lost. They believed she had most likely been abducted and they were determined to find her.

On Saturday, volunteers went to the Selma Flea Market and passed out missing person flyers. They spoke with vendors and customers at the market, hoping to find someone who might have seen Tarasha the previous week. According to Angela, "The family feels she did make it to the flea market. A couple of vendors said they saw her." Exactly what happened to her after she left remained a mystery.

That evening, a group of around 75 people gathered at Selma's Bloch Park to hold a candlelight vigil and prayer service for Tarasha. Regina was grateful to see how many people came out to show their support for her daughter. "Everybody has been sticking with me. That's what keeps me going."

As the investigation stretched into its second week, Detective Michael Ames admitted that they were running out of leads. "We need to hear from anybody who saw that gray Mazda between noon and 8:00 pm Saturday." Investigators were still trying to piece together exactly where Tarasha had gone when she left the flea market; they had received a few tips but "as far as locating her, we aren't any closer."

On July 6th, two search experts from the National Center for Missing and Exploited Children arrived in Selma to offer their assistance to the Selma detectives. They also met with members of Tarasha's family. Angela told reporters, "They have the expertise, so we are putting the search in their hands and in the hands of the Selma Police Department. We will continue to take information door-to-door."

Three weeks after Tarasha was last seen, there had been little progress in locating her. Selma Police Chief William Riley noted, "We're following up on any lead or idea that might be able to lead us to either a safe return of [Tarasha] or, if this turns into a recovery situation, to that." Bob Lowry, a spokesperson for the National Center for Missing and Exploited Children, reminded the public that the case was time-sensitive. "We think of time as the enemy. Someone out there knows what happened to this child and we need them to call."

The search effort was soon expanded to include much of Dallas County. Divers were sent into creeks and rivers, cadaver dogs combed through woods and fields, and helicopters searched from the air. Agencies from several surrounding counties assisted in the search, all of them hoping to be able to bring Tarasha home. Sadly, they found no clues as to what had happened to her.

Tarasha should have been celebrating her 18th birthday on September 16, 2010. Her loved ones marked the occasion with a small gathering at Bloch Park. Those in attendance wore T-shirts with Tarasha's picture to remind the public that the teenager was still missing. Her aunt, Tosha Benjamin, admitted, "We don't know if she's alive or dead." Regina, however, was trying to remain positive. "I believe she is going to come home."

Tarasha's loved ones did everything they could to make sure that the public didn't forget that the teenager was still missing, but the case soon faded from the headlines. Tips dried up, and months went by without any updates from law enforcement. A year after Tarasha was last seen, Lt. Mike Harris admitted that investigators were no closer to determining what had happened to her than they had been on the day she went missing. "Of course it's discouraging, because we want to know where this child is at and what happened to her." He made another appeal for anyone with information to contact the Selma Police Department, but no new leads were developed.

Tarasha's case remained cold until September 2016, when police received a tip that her body was buried behind an abandoned building that had once housed the Top Class Lounge. Investigators with the Alabama State Bureau of Investigations used ground penetrating radar to search the area and identified a couple of anomalies they believed could possibly be graves; they spent several days digging up the backyard with a backhoe but found nothing. The case went cold once more.

It's been nearly 13 years since Tarasha left to go to the flea market and never returned, and her disappearance continues to baffle the Selma Police Department. Regina believes that Tarasha could be a victim of sex trafficking and was likely taken out of the Selma area shortly after she went missing. There have been a few reported sightings of her in Florida; family members have traveled to Florida several times to follow up on these potential sightings but have never been able to confirm them. Regina feels that Tarasha is still alive and continues to search for her. "I never felt death with her...I can feel things with my kids. I tell people that all the time. I will never give up."

Tarasha Benjamin was 17 years old when she went missing from Selma, Alabama in June 2010. A friendly teenager with a ready smile, Tarasha loved going to the Selma Flea Market to search for bargains. Tarasha has black hair and brown eyes, and at the time of her disappearance, she was 5 feet 2 inches tall and weighed 125 pounds. She was last seen wearing blue shorts, a yellow, white, and turquoise striped shirt, silver sandals, and a silver necklace. Her ears are pierced and she has a tattoo of her nickname "Pooh" on her upper right arm. If you have any information about Tarasha, please contact the Selma Police Department at 334-874-2134.

Regina Bos

Regina Bos spent the evening of Monday, October 16, 2000, doing one of her favorite things: playing guitar and singing at an open mike night at Duggan's Pub in Lincoln, Nebraska. The 40-year-old was a regular at the pub; she had worked there off and on for four years and was friendly with many of the locals who frequented the place. Gina finished her set around 10:30 pm but lingered at the pub for a few hours afterward, chatting with friends and just having a good time.

Around 1:00 am, Gina packed up her guitar and several patrons recalled seeing her leave the bar and head for her car. It was the last time any of them would ever see her. Somehow, just steps away from Duggan's Pub, Gina vanished without a trace.

Gina's boyfriend of three months, Michael Johnson, had originally planned to go to Duggan's Pub with her that night. He changed his mind at the last minute, opting to go home and rest. Gina told him that she would pick him up when she left the pub so the two of them could spend the night at her house.

Michael dozed off while waiting for Gina. He woke up briefly around midnight, then went back to sleep, assuming that he would wake up when she knocked on his door. When he woke up again a couple of hours later, he realized that Gina had never arrived. Concerned, he paged her a few times but she didn't call him.

Gina had left her pager at home that night, and when Michael started paging her it woke up her three children. Although her kids – aged 11, 13, and 15 – were old enough that Gina felt comfortable leaving them home alone for a few hours at a time, she never stayed out overnight. When they saw that their mother wasn't home, the kids were immediately concerned. They called their father, Tony Williams, and their maternal grandparents.

When Michael learned that Gina hadn't made it home, he knew something was wrong and called one of her close friends, Dani Krause. By 6:30 am, the two of them were driving around the streets of Lincoln, searching for any sign of Gina or her green Saturn. It didn't take them long to spot Gina's car; it was parked across the street from Duggan's Pub. As they approached the car, Michael and Dani noticed that the trunk wasn't fully closed.

Fearful for what might be inside, Michael cautiously opened the trunk and peered into it. He and Dani were relieved that Gina wasn't inside, but what they saw made their hearts sink: Gina's guitar and sheet music. Dani explained, "Her music and her guitar are an appendage to her...they're like her fourth child. Gina would never, ever leave her guitar unsecured. Ever." At that moment, Dani knew something was terribly wrong.

Michael called the Lincoln Police Department and reported Gina missing at 6:38 am. Police officers and search dogs immediately started conducting a search of the area surrounding Duggan's Pub but found nothing to indicate what had happened to Gina. By that afternoon, Lincoln Police Detective Greg Sorenson had been assigned to the case. He headed straight for Duggan's Pub and began looking for anyone who had seen Gina the night before.

Gina had been at Duggan's Pub two different times on Monday, first for a friend's baby shower that afternoon and then for the open mike night. She felt at home in the pub, a typical neighborhood hangout with concrete floors and drawings of rock artists decorating the wall next to the stage. Gina was in her element on the stage and regularly participated in open mike nights. Dani noted, "I called her a stage junkie. She loved to sing, she loved to shine her light."

One of the people who showed up to watch Gina sing that night was her ex-husband, Dave Bos. Although Gina and Dave had divorced a couple of years earlier, it was an amicable parting and they were on friendly terms. He spoke with her for a few minutes that night, recalling, "She was in a real good mood. She loved to sing in front of people." Dave left shortly after Gina finished her set around 10:30 pm; Gina was still happily chatting with friends at the time.

Several of the bar patrons recalled seeing Gina leaving the bar around 1:00 am. One of the bar employees, a 61-year-old man, told detectives that when he left the bar shortly after 1:00 am, he saw Gina walking towards her car with her guitar case slung across her back. He headed in the opposite direction, so he didn't see if she made it to her car or not but he didn't hear yelling or anything to indicate she was in trouble.

It appeared that Gina had made it safely to her car, then unlocked the trunk and carefully laid her prized guitar inside. Investigators theorized that she was then approached by someone; this would explain why she never closed the trunk of her car. Since no one reported hearing any sounds of a struggle, it was unlikely that Gina was forcibly abducted. Detectives believed Gina knew the person who approached her and went with them willingly. What happened after that was a complete mystery.

Gina was one of seven siblings – she had four

sisters and two brothers – and none of them believed that she had disappeared voluntarily. As soon as they learned that she was missing, they immediately gathered in Lincoln to search for Gina. They printed and distributed thousands of missing person flyers and appealed to the local news media for help spreading the word about their missing sister.

By Friday, there had been no progress on the case and Gina's family was growing desperate to find her. Her sister, Jannel Rap, told a reporter, "We're looking under every stone. We're not giving up." She was certain that Gina had been a victim of foul play. "My sister loves and adores her children and would never take off. She would not worry her family this way."

On Saturday, 78,000 people attending a University of Nebraska game learned about Gina, as her picture and description were shown on the HuskerVision screens at Memorial Stadium. Announcers asked people to keep an eye out for the missing woman and to call police immediately if they had any information about her.

Detectives had interviewed dozens of people and were following up on each tip they received, but they admitted that they still weren't sure what had happened to Gina. Lincoln Police Captain Gary Engel told reporters, "We have a couple of people that we are running down to see what they have to say about her. I wouldn't call them suspects." Detective Sorenson clarified this, stating that "anybody could be a suspect at this time because we have absolutely no idea what happened."

One thing the detectives and Gina's loved ones agreed on was the fact that Gina was missing under extremely suspicious circumstances. Captain Engel noted, "Every day that goes by concerns us because the issue of foul play becomes more plausible." The family feared the worst. Jannel was honest about the chances of finding Gina alive. "She could be unconscious somewhere, she could have amnesia...either of these are a possibility. A slim possibility."

Hoping to raise money for a reward, Gina's family created T-shirts with her picture and information and sold them in the Lincoln area. On November 3, 2000, they held a fundraiser at the 1st Avenue Social Hall, featuring live music from various local bands. They were hopeful that someone with information would be enticed to come forward by a monetary reward, but none of the tips that were received led to Gina.

As weeks went by, Gina's family did everything they could to keep her name in the media. With no solid leads, it was hard to not get discouraged. Gina's brother, Kevin Rap, admitted, "We really don't know which direction to go now."

In November, Lamar Outdoor Advertising donated a dozen billboards to the search effort, and Gina's face was seen throughout the city of Lincoln. Friends and family members continued to distribute missing person flyers, both in Lincoln and across the country with the help of a network of long-haul truckers.

Gina should have been celebrating her 41st birthday on November 4, 2000. Her loved ones bought her birthday cards as they did each year, praying that she would be home to read them. Sadly, the day passed with no news about Gina.

As the holidays approached, the pain of missing Gina only intensified for her family. Her three children were spending the holiday with their father, Tony, and his family; they were careful to shield the three kids from the news media. Tony told reporters that the children were doing about as well as could be expected under the circumstances but they missed their mother. "They know that they are taken care of and they can talk about it anytime they want."

Gina's parents, Carlos and Dee Rap, dreaded the thought of spending Christmas without Gina. Carlos noted, "You feel like part of you is missing because part of you is. I don't know how to explain it...the best Christmas present would be to find Gina." His wife echoed the sentiment. "There's just an empty place."

As a way of honoring Gina and keeping the case in the public eye, Gina's family placed a billboard across the street from Duggan's Pub. It was put up just steps away from where Gina's car had been parked on the night she vanished and displayed a simple message: "We Miss You, Gina. Merry Christmas."

Months went by and Gina's fate remained unknown. For Jannel, the uncertainty was brutal. "That's the worst part of the whole thing, all the scenarios that go through your head." She just wanted to be able to bring her sister home and obtain some measure of closure.

Although detectives still had no evidence pointing directly to foul play, after interviewing everyone associated with Gina, they didn't believe she left of her own volition. In the days leading up to her disappearance, Gina had been very happy with her life. Her relationship with Michael was going well, she was scheduled to move into a new home provided by Habitat for Humanity, and she had recently started a new job that she loved. According to Dani, "She was ecstatic...she was the best I had ever seen her." There was simply no way she would have walked away from her life.

Investigators continued to follow up on each tip they received, but they were unable to develop any solid leads to help them find Gina. On October 16, 2001, Gina's loved ones gathered across the street from Duggan's Pub to hold a candlelight vigil. They taped a poster to a tree located next to where Gina's car had been parked to remind the public that they were still searching for the missing woman.

Captain Engel assured reporters that detectives did not consider Gina's case to be cold, though few tips were being called in. "By no means have we forgotten about this case...anybody who thinks they might have the slightest piece of information about her or her disappearance, it would certainly be good if they called us." Gina's mother also spoke to reporters at the vigil, stating, "We want people to know she's still out there somewhere. And we'd like people to keep looking."

Another year passed and Gina was still missing. Detectives had followed up on more than 500 tips in Nebraska and several adjacent states but remained baffled by the disappearance. For Gina's family, the second anniversary was no easier than the first had been. Dee told reporters, "If it wasn't for our faith, we just wouldn't make it."

By 2005, Gina had been missing for five years and her case had long since faded from the headlines. Once again, the family marked the grim anniversary of her disappearance by holding a vigil across the street from Duggan's Pub. Dee brought a poster with a picture of her daughter and the words "Bring me home. It's been five long years."

Although Gina was still classified as a missing person, Detective Sorenson admitted that he didn't believe she was still alive and he was investigating the case as if it was a homicide. He told reporters that he believed he knew who killed Gina – and had spoken to this person – but refused to provide any further details.

Five more years passed. Gina had been missing for a decade and her case, though still open, had stalled years earlier. Detective Sorenson said his top priority was proving who killed Gina and putting him in jail.

In the summer of 2015, Carlos and Dee Rap celebrated their 60th wedding anniversary. It should have been a happy occasion, but it was marred by the fact that Gina wasn't there to celebrate with them. Jannel noticed that Carlos seemed to be particularly emotional that year. "My dad's been kind of teary lately. He said, 'We have to do something for Gina.'" Jannel and her siblings took these words to heart and decided it was time to finally hold a memorial service for Gina.

Friends and family members gathered in Lincoln on September 12, 2015, to hold Gina's Celebration of Life. No one believed that there was any chance of finding Gina alive, but they were still determined to bring her home. Jannel told reporters, "Just because we're doing a celebration of life doesn't mean we are going to stop looking or stop trying to find out what happened to her."

Detective Sorenson retired from the Lincoln Police Department in 2016 and took a job with the county attorney's office. He continued to follow up on leads in Gina's case; he had worked the case since the day she was reported missing and wanted more than anything to obtain justice for Gina. "There are persons of interest who are considered suspects, but there is not enough evidence or probable cause to make an arrest." He – and Gina's loved ones – remain hopeful that someone will come forward with the information needed for them to finally bring Gina home.

Regina Bos was 40 years old when she went missing from Lincoln, Nebraska in 2000. She was a talented singer and guitar player, a beloved daughter and sibling, and a fantastic mother to three children. Gina has brown eyes and auburn hair, and at the time of her disappearance, she was 5 feet 6 inches tall and weighed 105 pounds. She was last seen wearing black pants, a black shirt, and black boots. She has a tattoo of a yellow rose on her back and her ears are pierced multiple times. If you have any information about Gina's case, please contact the Lincoln Police Department at 402-441-7706.

Jody Brant

Jody Brant wasn't a typical teenager. When the 16-year-old decided she wanted to visit family in Michigan over Memorial Day weekend in 1994, she didn't bother to ask anyone for permission. She simply packed a couple of suitcases, climbed into her black Ford Escort, and left her Lawrenceville, Georgia home to make the 770-mile drive north. It was a trip she made several times in the past, but on this occasion, something went horribly wrong. Jody never arrived at her cousin's house in Pontiac, Michigan and she was never seen again.

Although she was only 16 years old, Jody was very independent. Her mother, Donna, struggled with drug addiction and her father had never been a part of her life; Jody had learned to be self-sufficient at an early age. She had grown up in Michigan and remained close with friends and family there after moving to Georgia with her mother and older brother a couple of years earlier.

Jody worked full-time at a fast food restaurant and had been thrilled when she saved up enough money to buy a used Ford Escort. Her brother, Joseph, had helped her install a new stereo system in the car; it helped to keep her entertained on long trips. She put it to good use when she made the drive from Georgia to Michigan.

Jody left her home around 11:00 pm on Friday, May 27, 1994; she planned to drive through the night and hoped to reach Pontiac late the next morning. Although the drive was a long one, it was very straightforward; Interstate 75 went directly from Lawrenceville to Pontiac.

Jody called her cousin, Jennifer Jones, at her home in Pontiac around 10:00 am Saturday and told her that she had gotten lost near Erie, Michigan, a small town located around 10 miles north of Toledo, Ohio. Although her exact location was unclear, it appeared that Jody had accidentally gotten off Interstate 75 as it passed through Toledo. Her cousin gave her directions and assumed that she would soon be back on course. It was the last time Jennifer would hear from Jody.

When Jody failed to show up by Saturday afternoon, Jennifer knew that something had to be wrong. At 11:00 pm, she called both the Michigan State Police and the Ohio State Police and reported Jody missing. She told investigators that she wasn't sure if Jody had made it to Michigan or not; when she spoke to her at 10:00 am she had still been in Ohio. Jennifer believed Jody had been alone when she spoke with her and there had been no indication that she was in any kind of trouble. "She just sounded frustrated, like she was lost."

Jennifer called Jody's family in Georgia to let them know that the teenager had gone missing. Jody's uncle, Roy Jones, and her brother, Joseph, immediately drove from Georgia to Michigan, scouring Interstate 75 for any sign of Jody or her car. They stopped at gas stations and rest stops, hanging up missing posters and asking employees if any of them remembered seeing the teenager.

A gas station attendant at a Toledo-area service station told them that she was pretty sure she had seen Jody early Saturday morning; she claimed the teen used the payphone to make a phone call and purchased $10 worth of gas before leaving. This would be the last confirmed sighting of Jody.

As Roy and Joseph made their way to Michigan,

they had no idea that Jody's car had already been found. A resident of Ottawa Lake, Michigan called police around 7:00 am Sunday when they discovered a car that had been abandoned and set on fire near the intersection of Turk and Consear Roads. Deputies from the Monroe County Sheriff's Office responded to the call but didn't realize at the time that car was associated with a missing person.

It wasn't until Wednesday that the Michigan State Police connected the burned car and Jody's missing person report. They immediately launched an extensive search of the area where the car had been found, hoping to find some clue that might point to Jody's whereabouts. Troopers scoured the surrounding area on foot using search dogs, while a state police helicopter conducted an aerial search. They found no sign of Jody.

Detectives canvassed the neighborhood where the car had been abandoned, but none of the residents recalled hearing or seeing anything unusual that weekend. One homeowner pointed out that her dog, which would normally bark loudly when there were strangers in the vicinity, had been quiet the entire night. No one had any idea when the car had been ditched there.

Jody's car was processed by arson investigators with the Michigan State Police. They determined that the car had been set on fire sometime after 10:00 pm Saturday; it had been started on the floor by the front passenger seat. The keys had been left in the ignition and Jody's personal belongings, including her two suitcases, were found in the trunk.

When Jody's relatives saw her car, they noticed that there was a large dent in the rear bumper that hadn't been there when Jody left for her road trip. It looked as if she had been hit from behind; her mother was convinced that she had been purposely hit by someone who then abducted her when she pulled over to check the damage.

Another concerning detail about the car was the fact that the driver's seat had been pushed all the way back as if someone tall had been driving it. Jody was tiny and had to pull the seat all the way forward in order to reach the pedals; her family believed that someone else – someone much taller than Jody – had driven the car to the remote location where it was found.

Detectives interviewed all of Jody's known associates in both Georgia and Michigan. None of her friends or relatives in Michigan had spoken to her after 10:00 am Saturday, but a friend in Georgia told investigators that Jody had left a message on her answering machine at 6:00 pm Saturday. The message had been brief; Jody simply said she had made it to Pontiac and she was okay. It seemed odd that she hadn't contacted anyone in Michigan, and there was no solid evidence that she had ever made it to Pontiac that night.

When asked about the phone call Jody supposedly made, Pontiac Police Sgt. Everett Gard noted, "We believe it's possible she is alive and in the Pontiac area because of that last telephone message…[but] she may have been forced to make that last call, that's what we don't know."

Jody's stepfather, Robin Gulley, was perplexed by the message. "That doesn't make any sense. Why would she call a friend to say she was okay and not her mother or me?" He was certain that Jody met with foul play. "I have little doubt she's being held against her will. I think she was abducted by someone after she got off the phone after calling her cousin from Toledo." Still, the call gave him hope that Jody was still alive, and he told a reporter, "This story will have a good ending. I refuse to give up."

Jody's mother, Donna, refused to even contemplate the fact that Jody might have been killed.

Desperate to find her daughter, she consulted a psychic who told her that Jody was still alive and being held against her will somewhere in Michigan. Donna clung tightly to this idea. "I know she's alive." She made a public appeal for Jody's abductor to release her. "We're hoping if someone has her alive, they'll have a conscience. I just hope and pray they'd rather face kidnapping and arson charges instead of murder."

A week after Jody was last seen, her family announced that they were offering a $25,000 reward for information leading to Jody's recovery. A few people called in to report potential sightings of the missing teenager, but none of them could be confirmed.

There were rumors that Jody had been involved with drugs and this could have led to her disappearance, but there is no real evidence of this. Her stepfather told reporters that Jody had driven to Pontiac to deliver marijuana the week before she went missing, claiming "she had been talked into a delivery of drugs." This could be true – there was evidence that Jody and two male friends had made a trip to Pontiac earlier in May 1994, but there is nothing to suggest that Jody had any drugs with her when she went missing.

According to her stepfather's mother, Betty Gulley, Jody was just going to Michigan to visit her cousin over Memorial Day weekend. "She was going to stay there for a week and then they were going to come back together." The items found in Jody's car back up the assertion that she was going to Michigan for a vacation; in addition to her two suitcases filled with clothing, she had also packed her roller skates.

The Pontiac Police Department, the Michigan State Police, and the FBI were all involved in the initial stages of the investigation into Jody's disappearance. Despite the fact that there was no evidence Jody made it to Pontiac, it was decided that the Pontiac police would be the lead agency on the case.

The Michigan State Police continued to assist the Pontiac Police Department in their investigation into Jody's disappearance, but they weren't nearly as optimistic about the chances of finding her alive. Detective Sgt. Alison Hegwood noted, "We have a disappearance and a vehicle that has been burned. I'd say those are rather suspicious circumstances...we're treating this as a homicide until we get further information."

Unfortunately for investigators, they would never get any further information. Jody's trail went cold after she left the Toledo-area gas station that Saturday morning. Detectives believe that she was most likely a victim of foul play but exactly what happened to her remains a mystery.

Jody Lynn Brant was just 16 years old when she went missing in May 1994. Her older brother, Joseph, described her as being a spunky free spirit who was both tough and playful; she was mature for her age and was on the road to becoming a successful and responsible young adult. Jody has blonde hair and green eyes, and at the time of her disappearance, she was 5 feet 3 inches tall and weighed 120 pounds. She has a tattoo of her initials on her left hand and a cross on her left ankle. If you have any information about Jody, please contact the Michigan State Police at 734-242-3500.

Leonard Dirickson

Leonard Dirickson and his son, Jared, had just finished eating breakfast around 9:00 am on Saturday, March 14, 1998, when an unexpected visitor in a white pickup truck pulled up in their driveway. Jared watched through the window as his father went outside and approached the driver's side of the truck and spoke to the man behind the wheel for a few seconds. He then returned to the house and told Jared that he was going with the man, who wanted to buy one of his horses. He promised his son he would be back that afternoon, then climbed into the truck with the unidentified driver. The 39-year-old never returned home and was never seen again.

Leonard and his son lived on an 800-acre ranch in Strong City, Oklahoma, where they raised pigs and cattle. Leonard also owned 15 horses; he kept most of them in Elk City, Oklahoma, but also had at least one at a stud ranch in Mobeetie, Texas. When he left the house that Saturday morning, he told his son that he and the unidentified man were going to both locations.

When Leonard didn't come home that night, Jared started to get worried. He was just 16 years old at the time, and he and Leonard had an extremely close relationship. He was certain that his father would have called him if he was going to be away from home overnight. Worried that something might have happened to him, Jared called Leonard's parents, who lived in Elk City. When Leonard hadn't gotten in touch with anyone by the following morning, his parents called the Roger Mills

County Sheriff's Department and reported him missing.

Jared told police that his father had left with a white male driving a mid-1990s model white Ford 150 extended cab pickup truck. The truck had what Jared thought was a yellow New Mexico license plate on the front bumper, but New Mexico didn't issue front plates at the time so it was likely from a different state.

Since the man had never gotten out of his truck, Jared was unable to get a good look at him but believed he had a reddish-brown beard. It was unclear if Leonard had known the man, but he seemed at ease when he left and Jared didn't get the sense that he felt he was in any danger. Jared had wanted to accompany his father and the man, but Leonard had said he needed Jared to go to a local feed store and get feed for their pigs; the store closed at noon on Saturdays and Leonard knew he wouldn't be back before then.

Because the disappearance was so out of character for Leonard, police took the case seriously from the start. Worried that he and the unknown man might have been involved in a car accident, they scoured all the routes from Leonard's home to both Elk City and Mobeetie, both from the ground and from the air. They found nothing to indicate that the truck had been involved in a wreck or had run off the road.

Investigators searched Leonard's property and found a discarded Marlboro Light cigarette butt near the driveway. It was assumed to have belonged to the mystery man who picked Leonard up Saturday morning, but it didn't bring them any closer to learning his identity.

As word got out that Leonard was missing, a waitress at the Kettle Diner in Elk City called police to report seeing him and another male in the diner around 11:00 am Saturday. Although she didn't know Leonard personally, she was certain that it was him; Leonard had a very distinctive handlebar mustache that made him easily recognizable.

The waitress described Leonard's companion as a white man who appeared to be about 40 years old. The man had brown hair and a reddish-brown beard; he was 6 feet 2 inches tall and weighed around 210 pounds. He had been wearing a Western-style striped shirt, blue jeans, a blue jacket, and a black baseball cap with "No Fear" written on it in red. The waitress's description was detailed enough that a sketch artist was able to create a composite sketch of the man last seen with Leonard.

Leonard was the first person to go missing in Roger Mills County since 1981, and detectives were determined to find him. They distributed missing person posters throughout western Oklahoma and parts of Texas; in addition to a photograph of Leonard, the posters also included the sketch of the man who picked him up that Saturday morning. Although investigators received a few tips from people who thought they had seen Leonard, none of the sightings could be confirmed.

Investigators were perplexed by the disappearance. Roger Mills County Sheriff Joe Hay was blunt when he spoke to reporters about the case. "This is very unusual for this guy. Occasionally, you have a guy who twists off and goes away for a while, but that's not this guy. He's not a drinker and not a druggie. He's a hardworking guy."

Neighbors in Strong City told detectives that there was no way Leonard would have left his son alone for an extended period of time. None of them had ever seen the man in the white pickup truck before, but detectives believed that Leonard must have known him. "Leonard's house wasn't one you drive by, it was one you drove to…I'm not even sure you can see it from the road." To the sheriff, it was clear that the man had visited Leonard for a reason, but he wasn't sure it had anything to do with horses; investigators had learned that Leonard had never advertised any of his horses for sale.

The Oklahoma State Bureau of Investigation soon joined in the search for Leonard. Detectives followed up on each tip they received, but none of them led them any closer to finding the missing man. Sheriff Hay told reporters that he felt like he was chasing a ghost. "With most investigations, you usually have a place to start. We don't even know where to start with this one."

Hoping to find some clues, detectives probed into Leonard's past. He had married Kathy, his high school sweetheart, at the age of 18. They started running a dairy business on the Strong City ranch and soon had two children, Jared and Connie. The marriage eventually fell apart, however, and they divorced in 1996. It was an acrimonious split, and Leonard and Kathy were soon embroiled in a bitter custody battle that split their family in half. Kathy was granted custody of Connie and moved to Hammond, Oklahoma; Jared refused to live with his mother and remained on the ranch with Leonard.

In December 1997, Leonard made the difficult decision to sell the family's dairy business, although not because of the divorce. The cost of cattle feed increased drastically while the price of milk decreased, making it financially impossible for Leonard to maintain the business.

In January 1998, Leonard started a job with a metal company in Elk City. He ended up loving the job, so much so that his father, Don Dirickson, was thinking about purchasing the company for him. Unfortunately, Leonard vanished before Don could finalize these plans.

Although Leonard had faced some financial difficulties due to the loss of his dairy business, he seemed to be in a better position once he started working at the metal company and his son was unaware of any plans he had to sell any of his horses. As far as detectives could tell, Leonard had never advertised any horses for sale.

Dixie Gilworth, Leonard's aunt, described her nephew as an extremely nice person who wasn't afraid of hard work. "He's a dependable, capable guy. It just doesn't add up that he would leave with just the clothes on his back." Although she hoped that Leonard was still alive, she feared that the mysterious stranger had a sinister motive when he arrived at Leonard's ranch.

During the first few weeks of the investigation, detectives received hundreds of tips but were unable to develop any substantial leads concerning Leonard's whereabouts. They interviewed more than 70 people and were unable to find anyone who had anything bad to say about the missing man. Sheriff Hay noted, "We've talked to anyone and everyone he had dealings with and everyone thought the world of him. I'm sure there are a few out there who weren't his friend, we just haven't found them yet."

Family members stated that Leonard rarely carried more than $100 in cash on him, making him an unlikely target for robbery. He had maxed out all of his credit cards following his divorce, and his checking account was untouched. He hadn't made any substantial withdrawals in the weeks leading up to his disappearance, and his last paycheck hadn't been cashed.

No one who knew Leonard believed that he would have staged his own disappearance; he was far too close to his son to do that. None of his belongings were missing from his home and he didn't have the financial resources to simply start over somewhere else. They were convinced that he had been a victim of foul play.

Detectives believed that the unidentified man held the key to finding Leonard, but no one seemed to know who he was. None of Leonard's neighbors, friends, or family members recognized the man depicted in the sketch; they thought it likely the man was a stranger to Leonard as well. Although some questioned whether Leonard would have willingly gotten into a truck with someone he didn't know, Sheriff Hay noted, "Out here, where Leonard was born and raised, it comes natural to trust people." It was possible Leonard's trust had gotten him into trouble.

The first real lead in the case came in September 1998, when a man who claimed to know Leonard called the Oklahoma State Bureau of Investigation from a bar in Amarillo, Texas, and claimed that Leonard was at the bar. Authorities in Texas went to the bar but were unable to find Leonard or the man who made the phone call. They spent several nights staking out the bar to see if Leonard showed up but never saw any sign of him.

By the end of the year, the case had faded from the headlines. Jared, still not speaking with his mother, moved in with his grandparents in Elk City. He found some comfort in the fact that their home was filled with pictures of Leonard, and he continued to hope that his father would be found alive.

Leonard's parents, Don and Norma, wanted to believe that Leonard was still alive but admitted that it was a long shot. They were certain that he would have called Jared if he were able to, and the fact that there hadn't been any word from him indicated that he was most likely dead. Norma told a reporter, "In my heart, I know something bad has happened. He wouldn't have left

Jared. They were just too close."

As time went on, Sheriff Hay admitted that he had no idea what had happened to Leonard. Although family members were certain that Leonard wouldn't have staged his own disappearance, investigators had been unable to find any concrete evidence of foul play. "We don't know if he's still alive, but I'm convinced that he's still out there somewhere." The fact that his body had never been found meant there was still a chance he was alive.

Leonard's parents clung to this hope. In 2000, Don told a reporter, "If he's alive, I just want him to come back home. Jared needs him worse than we do." As more time went by, it got harder for Don and Norma to stay positive.

Detectives continued to circulate the composite sketch of the man last seen with Leonard but no one was able to identify him. Although Leonard's family expressed some doubt about the validity of the sighting that led to the sketch – they questioned whether Leonard would have gone to a diner to eat so soon after eating breakfast with his son – detectives still think that finding the man in the sketch is the key to solving this case.

Leonard Neal Dirickson was 39 years old when he went missing in 1998. The circumstances surrounding his disappearance have led authorities to suspect that he was a victim of foul play, but they admit that it's possible he vanished voluntarily. His family doesn't believe that he would have abandoned his teenage son, who still hopes to reunite with his father. Leonard has gray eyes and brown hair, and at the time of his disappearance, he was 5 feet 10 inches tall and weighed approximately 200 pounds. When he was last seen, Leonard was wearing green jeans, a faded black hooded Carhartt jacket, and a brown baseball cap with a green bill with "ACCO FEEDS" written on it. If you have any information about Leonard, please contact the Oklahoma Bureau of Investigation at 800-522-8017.

Lauren Dumolo

Lauren Dumolo often started her day with a meditation session at Four Freedoms Park near her home in Cape Coral, Florida. The morning of Friday, June 19, 2020, was no different. The 29-year-old left her apartment on Coronado Parkway around 8:00 am headed for the park on foot, a walk that usually took her around six minutes. What happened after that is a mystery; Lauren hasn't been seen since.

Lauren's boyfriend, Gabriel Pena, was surprised when he arrived at Lauren's apartment at 10:00 pm that night and found it empty. He grew concerned when he realized that Lauren's cell phone was sitting on her kitchen table; it was unusual for her to go anywhere without it. According to Gabriel, he tried to call the Cape Coral Police Department and report Lauren missing but was told he needed to wait 48 hours before he could file a report. Unsure what to do next, at 11:00 pm he called Lauren's father.

Paul Dumolo was surprised when he answered his phone and heard Gabriel's voice, as he lived in California and had never met his daughter's boyfriend. At first, he wasn't too concerned; he assumed that Lauren would be quickly located. "I just thought she must be at her mom's house or the store or something."

By the next day, Lauren was still missing and Paul realized that the situation was more serious than he initially thought. He told Gabriel to call police and insist on filing a missing person report, then booked a flight from

California to Florida. He arrived on Sunday and was dismayed to learn that Gabriel had not reported Lauren missing. Paul immediately went to the Cape Coral Police Department and filed a report.

Unbeknownst to Lauren's loved ones, her purse and shoes had been found in Four Freedoms Park Friday afternoon but since no missing person report had been filed at the time police were unaware of their importance. It wasn't until Paul arrived at the police station that investigators realized the significance of the find. Lauren's wallet and keys were found inside her purse; wherever Lauren was, she had no access to money. Authorities immediately launched a search for the missing woman.

Police combed through Four Freedoms Park with search dogs but found no trace of Lauren. By June 24th, investigators were concerned enough that they upgraded Lauren's status to that of an endangered missing person, though they wouldn't comment on the reason behind the change. They made several public appeals for help in determining Lauren's whereabouts, asking anyone who had seen her on June 19th or after to contact detectives.

Gabriel told investigators that he had stayed at Lauren's apartment on the night of June 18th; he left for work at 6:00 am on the 19th and Lauren was still asleep at that time. A maintenance worker at the Coronado Apartment complex reported seeing Lauren at 8:15 am; he remembered her because she had asked him if he knew of any cheaper apartments in the area. She mentioned wanting to "get out of the situation she was in" but it was unclear exactly what she meant by this.

Lauren had attempted to make a video call to Gabriel at 10:00 am on Friday; Gabriel didn't answer the call and told investigators that he had been at work and hadn't heard it come in. This call would be the last time

Lauren's cell phone was used.

Several organized searches of Four Freedoms Park failed to yield any useful information about what might have happened to Lauren. In an effort to solicit tips, Southwest Florida Crimestoppers announced that they were offering a $3,000 reward for information regarding Lauren's disappearance. Disappointingly, only a handful of tips were received.

The first new piece of physical evidence was found on July 2nd, when a shirt believed to belong to Lauren was recovered in Four Freedoms Park. Oddly, it was found in an area that had been searched several times before, leading some to speculate that it had been planted there. Forensic testing confirmed that the shirt was Lauren's, but it contained no clues about what might have happened to her.

Desperate to find Lauren, her friends and family members did everything they could to make sure that the public was aware she was still missing. They made missing person flyers and distributed them throughout Lee County, knocking on doors and speaking with residents to see if any of them might have seen the missing woman. They turned all potential tips over to investigators, who followed up on each one. None led them any closer to Lauren, leading her father to ruefully note, "She pretty much vanished."

In the weeks leading up to her disappearance, Lauren had been dealing with some mental health issues that made finding her even more of a priority. On two occasions – June 1st and June 15th – she had been involuntarily hospitalized under the Baker Act after she started exhibiting signs that she was in some kind of mental distress.

According to Paul, Lauren had no history of mental

illness prior to June 2020. Lauren's sister, Cassie, believed that Lauren was dealing with the aftershocks from a recent abortion. She noted, "When you hold in too much for too long, you're going to explode in some way." Lauren started hearing voices and told family members that she believed there were people after her.

She seemed to improve some after she was released from the hospital in early June. The week before she vanished, she and Gabriel had spent a day at the beach with Cassie and her two children. Cassie told reporters that the sisters had a great time that day and Lauren seemed to be in good spirits. She also noted that there hadn't appeared to be any problems between Lauren and Gabriel's relationship; they spent the day hugging and laughing like any happy couple.

Just two days after the sisters' beach trip, however, Lauren started once again showing signs of mental distress. She spoke with her father on the phone at that time and told him that she had no idea what was happening to her. She exhibited signs of paranoia and stated that she thought someone might be drugging her. She was hospitalized for the second time on June 15th.

Lauren was discharged from the hospital on June 18th and once again seemed to be in good spirits. Prior to her hospitalization, she had been working two jobs, one at a local Taco Bell and another at a small restaurant. Unfortunately, she lost both of these jobs – and her source of income – due to the fact that she had been in the hospital. Once she was discharged, she immediately set about trying to get her life back in order. She was seen on surveillance camera applying for a job at a local gas station that evening; nothing appeared to be wrong with her at that time.

All of Lauren's loved ones agreed that she was not

the type of person who would have voluntarily gone missing. She was close with her sisters and spoke to her father frequently. Although she had experienced some bumps in the road – a car accident when she was a teenager led to an opiate addiction that took her years to beat – she had been in recovery for two years at the time of her disappearance and was actively working to regain custody of her 5-year-old daughter, who was living with her maternal grandmother in West Palm Beach. She never would have willingly abandoned little McKayla.

There was little progress on the case over the next couple of months. Hoping to reinvigorate the investigation, an anonymous Marco Island businessman offered a $5,000 reward for information, bringing the total reward offered to $8,000. Sadly, the increased reward failed to bring in any new information.

By the end of August, Crimestoppers had received only a dozen or so tips, and none of them led to Lauren. Trish Routte, a manager for Crimestoppers, admitted that the lack of tips was disappointing. "It's sad and frustrating at the same time, because someone out there has to know something or have seen her after the morning of June 19th."

On September 3rd, Southwest Florida Crimestoppers asked for volunteers to help hand out more than 100 large yard signs with Lauren's picture and information about her case. Dozens of people helped, and soon the yard signs could be seen throughout Lee County. Lauren's family was humbled by the number of volunteers willing to help. Paul told reporters, "We are talking total strangers who never knew me or my daughter...it's heartwarming that there are still good people out there."

Hoping that a larger reward might entice someone with information to finally come forward, Lauren's loved ones decided to hold a fundraising event on October 3, 2020. Danielle Langevin, who hadn't known Lauren personally but felt compelled to help when she learned about the missing woman, was hopeful that the publicity about the case would compel the person or persons responsible for Lauren's disappearance to finally start talking. "We hope that they come forward...that the guilt will be too much and they will realize how much Lauren was loved."

The event, which was named "We Ride For Lauren", included a motorcycle ride led by Paul Dumolo as well as food, music, raffles, and auctions. The event was a success, with more than 60 motorcyclists participating in the ride. Dozens of local businesses donated money, auction items, and food for the event, which raised more than $6,000. Lauren's sister, Cassie, was pleased with the turnout and stated, "I hope this event will shed some light on what happened to her."

Although Lauren's loved ones tried to remain optimistic, the amount of time that had passed without any word from her was clearly affecting them. Her sister Lindsay noted, "Never in my wildest dreams could I think she could die this young, but I'm still hoping." Like Cassie, she hoped that raised awareness about the case would finally lead to some answers.

The family faced more heartbreak in October. On October 15th, Lauren's mother died after contracting COVID-19 while hospitalized with various other ailments, including kidney failure. Just four days later, Lauren's stepmother died. Paul fought through the pain, stating, "I am not giving up on looking for my daughter."

Cape Coral Master Cpl. Phillip Mullen admitted that Lauren's case was frustrating, noting, "Most missing person cases are resolved quickly." The department took a total of 18 missing person reports in June and July, and by August all the cases had been solved except for Lauren's.

Paul remained in constant contact with detectives but there was little they could tell him. He was convinced that Lauren had been abducted and either murdered or sexually trafficked and was growing desperate for some information about her whereabouts. "I wouldn't wish this on my worst enemy...you have this little bit of hope that she is still alive, but there is a chance she isn't alive and I think it's worse not knowing."

During the early stages of the investigation, Paul told reporters that he was sure detectives were doing everything they could to find Lauren but he was frustrated over the lack of progress. By November, he was getting tired of waiting for answers and decided to hire a private detective. Telling reporters that "Cape Coral Police Department can't find anything for whatever reason," Paul used $4500 of the money raised by the "We Ride For Lauren" event to hire private investigator Walt Zalisko.

PI Zalisko was blunt in his assessment of the case, noting that there had been no reported sightings of Lauren since she went missing. Her social media accounts, bank account, and credit cards remained untouched. It was as if she had vanished into thin air. "It's fair to say she is not with us anymore and it is a matter of finding her remains and the people involved."

On December 5th, Lauren's loved ones gathered in Four Freedoms Park to complete a one-mile walk in honor of Lauren. Before the event started, Cape Coral Police Chaplain Donald Neace said a prayer for Lauren and those searching for her. Family members, friends, police officers, and volunteers carried a banner with Lauren's picture on it during the walk, stopping frequently to tie pink ribbons around trees. It was their way of trying to raise awareness of the fact that Lauren was still missing and they were still desperate to find her. Cassie noted that the passage of time hadn't eased the pain of missing her sister. "You would think it would get easier but it's not. It is the same as Day 1."

Months passed with no progress on the investigation. On June 19, 2021, Lauren's family, along with friends, local residents, and Cape Coral police officers, gathered in Four Freedoms Park to mark the grim anniversary of her disappearance. It was an emotional time for the family as they tried to process the fact that a full year had gone by and they were no closer to finding Lauren. Paul told reporters, "I am at the point between anger, frustration, and heartbreak. The pain is there every single day."

To honor Lauren, her loved ones placed a bench near her favorite spot in Four Freedoms Park, a place where she had spent so many hours meditating about life. A small ceremony was held, with Cape Coral Fire Chaplain Mark Matthews saying a quick prayer and offering some words of encouragement to those still trying to process their loss. A plaque on the bench read, "Lauren is always with us, our angel, #bringlaurenhome."

Although Lauren's loved ones have never given up on finding her, the investigation into her disappearance has stalled. Cape Coral Police Detective Nick Jones told reporters that only a few tips were received in the case and there was no new information to report. Still, like Lauren's family, detectives remain optimistic. "We are still hopeful that someone in the community will come forward with information that will lead to a break in the case."

Lauren Dumolo was 29 years old when she went

missing from Cape Coral, Florida in June 2020. Her loved ones have been tirelessly searching for her ever since and will not give up until they can bring Lauren home. Lauren has brown eyes and brown hair, and at the time of her disappearance, she was 5 feet 1 inch tall and weighed 105 pounds. She has several tattoos, including the word "namaste" on her side, rosary beads on her ankle, "NY" on her pelvis, and the Om symbol on the inside of her wrist. If you have any information about Lauren, please contact the Cape Coral Police Department at 239-574-3223.

Jason Ellis

Jason Ellis was extremely close with his mother, Neatrice Billingsley. So when the 20-year-old suddenly stopped answering her phone calls in December 2006, his mother knew something was wrong. After more than a week without any word from Jason, Neatrice was concerned enough that she decided to drive to his home to check up on him.

Jason had moved out of the family's home in Merrillville, Indiana, several months before and was living with friends in Indianapolis, Indiana, but he called home frequently to speak to Neatrice. His last phone call had been on Sunday, December 3, 2006. His roommates, two of his friends from his high school days in Merrillville, had been out of town at the time so he had the townhouse to himself. Jason had seemed to be his usual cheerful self and his mother hadn't sensed that anything was wrong during the phone call; she had no idea that she would never speak to her son again.

When Jason's roommates arrived home a few days later, Jason wasn't there. At first, they weren't concerned; Jason had a habit of returning to Merrillville for a few days whenever he had any time off from work and they assumed that he would be back soon. They were surprised when Neatrice called looking for her son; they told her they thought he had gone to visit her.

By December 11, 2006, Neatrice was convinced that something was terribly wrong and made the 3-hour drive from Merrillville to Indianapolis to see if she could find her son. She was shocked to find his car parked outside of his townhouse; she knew there was no way Jason would have gone anywhere without his car.

What Neatrice found inside her son's room was even more concerning. All of his belongings appeared to have been left behind; the only thing that was missing was the comforter from his bed. Frightened, Neatrice called the Indianapolis Metropolitan Police Department and reported Jason missing.

If Neatrice had thought that the police would jump into action to help her find her son, she was sorely disappointed. Jason was an adult, and investigators told her that he was free to go missing if he wanted to. They took a brief look around his room and found no overt signs of foul play; the room was neat and there was no blood or signs of a struggle. Although Neatrice pointed out that her son's missing comforter likely indicated foul play, investigators shrugged it off. They told her that Jason had likely gone away with friends for a while and would probably be back soon.

Jason's loved ones knew that he wouldn't have gone anywhere without letting his mother know where he was going to be. He hadn't told anyone at work that he was going away, he had simply stopped showing up. His last two paychecks, which were deposited directly into his bank account, were untouched.

Neatrice realized that if she wanted her son found, it was up to her to find him. The heartbroken mother launched her own search for him, combing through the streets surrounding his townhouse. She peered into garbage cans and dumpsters with a sense of dread, wanting to find her son yet not wanting to find him dead.

Desperate to find her son, Neatrice made missing posters and hung them up throughout the Indianapolis area. She reached out to several local newspapers, begging them to write an article about Jason's disappearance, but none of them were interested.

In 2008, Jason's case found its way onto the desk of Indianapolis Metropolitan Police Detective Charles Gold. Unlike those who had handled the case before, Gold believed that Jason had likely been murdered. For the first time, Neatrice had an ally. Gold promised her that he would do everything he could to find her son.

It was a difficult investigation from the start. Jason had been missing for almost two years before Gold was assigned to the case, and the initial investigators hadn't made any real attempts at determining what had happened to the missing man. Gold interviewed Jason's family and friends in Merrillville but didn't come up with any solid leads.

Gold tried to interview people Jason had been associated with during his brief time in Indianapolis but found that many of them didn't want to talk to him. Many simply refused to answer his repeated knocks on their door, while others would open their door only to tell Gold that he would have to talk to their attorney. It was unclear if they were refusing to cooperate because they were involved in Jason's disappearance or if they simply didn't like police.

By 2010, Neatrice just wanted answers. She no longer cared if the person responsible for Jason's disappearance was ever held accountable; she just wanted to know where her son was. She was certain Jason had been murdered and told a reporter that she had a message for the killer. "If you can live with what you've done, the Almighty God can take care of the rest of it. It's not about vengeance. I simply want to know what happened to my child."

Detective Gold continued trying to find the answers Neatrice wanted, but admitted that the only way the case was likely to be solved was if Jason's body was found or if the killer came forward and confessed to police. Unfortunately, neither of these has happened.

Neatrice died in 2013 after suffering a massive brain hemorrhage, and many believed the stress of her son's disappearance was ultimately responsible for her death. Gold told a reporter, "She was an awesome lady." He was heartbroken that he hadn't been able to find Jason for her before she died, but hoped she was finally at peace. "They're together now. Maybe. Hopefully. I would like to think in my mind they are."

Jason Ellis was 20 years old when he went missing in 2006. Investigators believe that he was most likely murdered but have been unable to locate his body; until they do, a slim chance remains that he is still alive somewhere. Jason has brown eyes and black hair, and at the time of his disappearance, he was 6 feet 1 inch tall and weighed 160 pounds. He has a chipped front tooth and both of his ears are pierced. He has "Neatrice" tattooed on his chest, a maple leaf and his name tattooed on his right arm, and the cartoon characters Scrappy Doo and Scooby Doo tattooed on his left arm. If you have any information about Jason, please contact the Indianapolis Metropolitan Police Department at 317-327-6984.

-

Jared Hanna

Jared Hanna left his home in Jerseyville, Illinois around 11:30 am on Saturday, July 2, 2011. The 28-year-old was a single father of two, and much of his time was spent either working or taking care of his children. He had some time to himself this particular weekend because his daughters were visiting their mother in St. Louis, Missouri.

It's unclear exactly what Jared planned to do that Saturday. When he left his house he took his fishing gear and some bait with him, so it seems likely that he was going to spend at least part of the day fishing. When he didn't return home that night, his family wasn't immediately concerned. Jared had mentioned going on a possible camping trip at some point; they thought perhaps he had decided to do so that weekend.

The first hint that something might be wrong came around midnight on July 4th, when Jared's sister, Heather, got a call from Jared's ex asking if he was home. She told Heather that Jared was supposed to pick up his daughters at some point on Sunday night but had failed to do so and she had been unable to get a hold of him on his cell phone.

Jared's family was concerned but tried to remain positive. They hoped that Jared was still camping and had either lost track of time or was simply out of cell phone range and unable to notify anyone that he was running late. By Monday night, however, there was still no word from Jared and his family was getting increasingly worried with each passing hour.

On Tuesday, Jared's mother, Pat New, received a

phone call that seemed to confirm the family's fears that something had happened to Jared. The 1990 GMC Sierra Jared had been driving was found abandoned in a rural area of Clinton County, Illinois, roughly 70 miles from Jared's Jerseyville home.

A deputy with the Clinton County Sheriff's Department had first spotted the truck on the side of Jolliff Bridge Road when he was driving home early Sunday morning, but he hadn't really paid too much attention to it at the time. When he drove that way again on Tuesday and saw that the truck was still sitting in the same spot, the deputy decided to investigate to make sure it wasn't stolen. The truck was registered to Pat; when the deputy called her, he learned that her son had been driving the truck and was now missing.

As soon as Jared's family heard that his truck had been found abandoned, they filed a missing person report with the Clinton County Sheriff's Department. While officials with that department started investigating the area where the truck had been found, detectives with the Jersey County Sheriff's Department started trying to determine where Jared had gone after he left his home late Saturday morning.

Jared was seen on surveillance footage stopping at a Jerseyville Amoco station around 11:45 am on Saturday; he went inside, paid cash for a soda, and left. His cell phone pinged off a cell tower in East Alton, Illinois around 12:30 pm, indicating that Jared had headed south when he left the gas station. From there, he headed for the Centralia area. Around 9:30 pm, he called his ex-wife to check in on his daughters; he was still in Centralia at that time, though he didn't give his ex any details about what he was doing there.

Jared had once worked in Centralia and was

familiar with the area. According to his sister, some of Jared's old co-workers had told him about some private land there where he could go fishing; since Jared had his fishing gear with him when he left the house, it seems likely that he went to one of these fishing spots. Investigators went to each of the areas where he might have gone but were unable to find any clues to his whereabouts.

When Jared's truck was found, it was out of gas. Detectives assumed that Jared had set out on foot after running out of gas and canvassed the area looking for anyone who might have seen him. They found one potential witness who described seeing someone matching Jared's description walking along Jolliff Bridge Road early Sunday morning; since the witness said this person was carrying a gas can, investigators believed it was most likely Jared. Heather, however, isn't so sure. The witness stated that the man he saw was wearing a wifebeater, something that Heather said her brother never would have worn.

Residents of a trailer on College Road in Centralia claimed that a man they believed was Jared knocked on their door around 8:30 am Sunday and asked for directions to Casey's General Store, which was more than five miles away. They told detectives that the man also asked for a drink of water; he drank two glasses and then went on his way.

Jared's loved ones were adamant that he never would have disappeared voluntarily. He was a dedicated father to his two daughters and had a steady job. Although it wasn't easy being a single father, his family was very supportive and Heather watched the girls for him whenever he had to go out of town for work. His mother noted, "He wouldn't just leave, no matter how tough it was. He loved his girls more than anything."

Desperate to find Jared, his family made missing person flyers and spent Wednesday handing them out in Clinton County near where his truck had been found. They pleaded for anyone with any information to contact them or police.

The week passed without any word from Jared. On Saturday, July 9th, the family organized a search of the Jolliff Bridge Road area, hoping to find some clue as to what had happened to Jared. While volunteers searched the ground using ATVs and horses, an airplane flew overhead looking for anything they might have missed. They found no clues as to what had happened to Jared. Heather told reporters, "It isn't like my brother to just disappear...we're just really worried and want him home."

Jersey County Sheriff Mark Kallel admitted to reporters that they didn't have a lot of information to go on. "We are continuing our efforts...we're doing everything we can think of but we're not getting too far."

Cell phone records indicated that Jared hadn't used his phone since the night he went missing; it had last pinged off a cell tower in Centralia at 9:30 pm. After that, it had either been turned off or the battery had died, and investigators had been unable to ping its location. Search dogs had been brought to Jolliff Bridge Road but had been unable to pick up Jared's trail. Just a week into the investigation, the case was already in danger of going cold.

The lack of information was hard on Jared's loved ones. Pat admitted, "You just feel so lost, just helpless." Heather agreed. "We are exhausted and just emotionally drained right now...none of us are getting any sleep at all."

Two weeks into the investigation, little progress had been made. According to Clinton County Sheriff Mike Kreke, there had been no further sightings of Jared after he supposedly stopped and asked for water and directions. After that, his trail went cold. It would remain cold for the next three months.

On October 10, 2011, a black shoulder bag belonging to Jared was found on the banks of Crooked Creek, about a mile and a half away from where his truck had been found on Jolliff Bridge Road. The bag contained Jared's wallet, cell phone, video camera, tools, and keys; some of his clothing and a pair of shoes were found nearby. Family members positively identified the items as belonging to Jared.

The discovery of Jared's belongings jumpstarted the investigation. The Clinton County Sheriff's Department conducted a search of the Crooked Creek area; deputies, volunteers, and cadaver dogs spent hours combing along the creek bed and surrounding area but failed to find anything else related to the investigation.

By January 2012, the case had started to stall. In an effort to bring in some new tips, Clinton County Crimestoppers announced that they were offering a $5,000 reward for information leading to Jared. Clinton County Chief Deputy Sheriff Mark Etter noted, "We are hoping that this reward may bring someone forward so that we have a direction to focus our resources." Few tips came in, however, and the investigation soon went cold.

Jared's family marked the grim first anniversary of his disappearance in July 2012. The passage of time hadn't made dealing with his loss any easier; Pat told one reporter, "It's hard. We miss him and his girls miss him." Heather had taken on the responsibility of caring for Jared's two daughters in his absence; they were too young to fully comprehend the situation and still thought about their dad every day.

A candlelight vigil for Jared was held at Lion's Club

City Park in Jerseyville on July 2, 2012. Around 50 people gathered to honor Jared and remember the good times they had with him. Pat noted, "Are we worried? Most definitely. Do we want him home? Yes, 100 percent and we don't care how...we want closure. It will be total turmoil until the day we find him."

Detectives remained completely baffled by Jared's disappearance, but Chief Deputy Etter said he was hopeful that the publicity surrounding the anniversary would bring in some new leads. "We are doing all that we can and anytime we hear something, we check it out." Sadly, no new leads were developed.

Over the next decade, there would be a number of additional searches for Jared but no new evidence was found and his fate remained a mystery, with detectives unable to rule out any possible scenario in his disappearance.

Jared's family has always believed he was a victim of foul play, and they may be right. Oddly, Jared's truck wasn't initially kept as potential evidence and was immediately released to his family by the Clinton County Sheriff's Department. There were a couple of things about the truck that bothered Jared's loved ones. Although detectives believed that the truck had been abandoned after running out of gas, it started up immediately after Jared's family put some gas in it. According to a mechanic Heather spoke with, if the truck had truly run out of gas, it would have been impossible to start it without priming the gas pedal a few times to get the fuel back into the fuel system. Because of this, Jared's family believes that someone might have deliberately left the truck there and then siphoned the fuel out of the truck to make it look as if it had run out of gas.

Jared had his guitar and amplifier in his truck when

he went missing but they were no longer there when the truck was recovered and they have never been found. According to Heather, the inside of the truck looked as if it had been ransacked, making robbery a potential motive in the case.

Sadly, Jared's mother died in 2020 without learning what had happened to her beloved son. Heather, who adopted both of Jared's girls after his disappearance, has never stopped searching for her brother and is determined to learn what happened to him. She – and Jared's daughters, who are now teenagers – deserve answers.

Jared Hanna was 28 years old when he went missing from Centralia, Illinois in July 2011. He was a dedicated father of two young daughters and his family doesn't believe he willingly abandoned them. Jared has brown hair and brown eyes, and at the time of his disappearance, he was 5 feet 9 inches tall and weighed 195 pounds. He has a scar on the back of his head and one on the heel of his right foot. He was last seen wearing a T-shirt, jean shorts, and sneakers. If you have any information about Jared, please contact the Clinton County Sheriff's Department at 618-594-4555 or Clinton County Crimestoppers at 618-594-6666. A $5,000 reward is available for information leading to Jared's location or the arrest and conviction of the person responsible for his disappearance.

Khiara Henry

Khiara Henry had always wanted to go to Hawaii. In July 2019, she decided the time was right for an impromptu trip to the islands. On July 11, 2019, the 23-year-old flew from her hometown of San Diego to Hawaii. She spent a week at the Turtle Bay Resort on the island of Oahu, then flew to the island of Maui on July 17th. She checked out of her hotel in Kihei on July 21st, then rented a car and drove to Wai'anapanapa State Park in Hana. What happened to her after that is unclear; her rental car was found in a parking lot at the state park but Khiara has never been seen again.

Khiara was an adventurous and independent young woman who was used to traveling solo. She was alone when she checked into the Aston Maui Hills Resort in Kihei on July 18th, but she signed up for a couple of organized tours so she could do some sightseeing and meet some new people at the same time. She took a Hana Tours of Maui bus tour on July 19th, which included a stop at Wai'anapanapa State Park. On July 20th, she went on a Hike Maui tour of Wailele Farm – Twin Falls. Khiara had especially enjoyed seeing Wai'anapanapa State Park and decided she wanted to explore that area further.

On the morning of July 21st, Khiara used a computer at the Aston Maui Hills Resort to book a rental car for later that day. She made a reservation at the Sugar Beach Resort in Kihei for July 22nd through July 29th, then booked a flight back to San Diego on July 29th. She then checked out of the Aston Maui Hills Resort and took a cab to the Hertz rental car center at the Kahului airport in Maui County.

Khiara was alone when she arrived at the rental car agency and picked up a black Nissan Sentra. She confirmed with the clerk that she only needed the car for 24 hours and would be returning it the following day. She then got into her rental car and drove directly to Wai'anapanapa State Park, a 49-mile drive that took about two hours to make. From there, her trail goes cold.

Khiara was notoriously bad at keeping in touch with people when she was traveling. She didn't use social media and had a tendency to lose or break cell phones. Because of this, her family wasn't immediately concerned when they were unable to get a hold of her. Everything changed on July 26th, when a Hertz employee reached out to Khiara's older sister, Thea Hammond, and told her that Khiara had seemingly abandoned her rental car at Wai'anapanapa State Park with some of her belongings still inside.

A park ranger had first noticed the Nissan Sentra parked in one of the park's lots on July 23rd, but admitted that it could have been there for a couple of days at that point. Despite the fact that it didn't have a permit to park in the lot overnight, no action was taken until July 25th, when a park official called the Maui County Police Department and reported the car as abandoned.

Maui County officers determined that the car had been rented from Hertz and made arrangements to have it towed back to their agency. Even though the vehicle contained a number of Khiara's belongings – including her driver's license and her debit card – no attempt was made at locating her.

Once Hertz had possession of the car, they immediately had it washed and vacuumed so it would be ready to be rented out again. Khiara's belongings were turned over to the Maui County Police Department; no one from the department reached out to anyone from Khiara's family to check on her whereabouts.

A woman who worked for Hertz thought it was odd that officials didn't seem concerned about Khiara, so she took it upon herself to reach out to Khiara's older sister on Facebook and let her know what was going on. Thea and her parents immediately tried to contact Khiara, but her cell phone appeared to be turned off and all calls went straight to her voicemail. It was at this point that Khiara's family realized that something was wrong; they called the Maui County Police Department and reported Khiara as missing.

As soon as they realized that Khiara was missing, her parents and siblings flew to Maui to assist in the search for her. Initially, the Maui County police seemed to think that Khiara had gone missing voluntarily; it wasn't until July 28th that they released any information about the missing woman to the public and asked for help in locating her.

Khiara's family created a "Find Khiara Henry" Facebook page on July 28th and immediately started recruiting volunteers to help search for the missing woman. They made missing person posters and asked anyone who had visited Wai'anapanapa State Park on or after July 21st to contact them if they thought they had any information about Khiara.

The first organized search of the state park took place on July 30th. Members of Maui Search and Rescue used tracking dogs to search through the parking lots and along various trails but found no sign of the missing woman. Investigators interviewed employees and visitors, hoping to find someone who remembered seeing Khiara, but the transient nature of the state park made finding witnesses difficult.

Detectives determined that nearly everything Khiara had brought to Hawaii had been left in her rental car, including her luggage, debit card, and identification. It seemed unlikely that she would have been able to leave the island without these items, so her family was convinced she was still in the immediate area.

The only items that were not found in the rental car were Khiara's cell phone, the keys to the car, and a small black backpack that Khiara usually carried. Phone records showed that the cell phone had been turned off since July 21st, and Khiara had last used her debit card on that same day.

Wai'anapanapa State Park, located on the eastern coast of the island of Maui, is best known for its black sand beaches and rugged coastline. The 122-acre park sits near Hana, one of the most isolated communities on the island. It made sense that Khiara, who loved unplugging from technology and spending time outdoors, would be attracted to the park; she enjoyed hiking and had probably intended to follow some of the ancient trails along the Hana Highway. Her family worried that she might have been in some kind of accident and was lying somewhere, unable to call for help due to the fact that there was no cell phone service inside the park.

Khiara's mother, Monica Henry, expressed concern about all the unknowns in her daughter's disappearance. "We do not know if she went hiking or got lost in the park. We do not know if she went to meet somebody. We do not know if she picked up a hitchhiker or met with foul play in the parking lot." There were no surveillance cameras in the state park, so it was impossible to determine exactly when Khiara arrived and if she had been alone at the time.

One thing seemed clear: Khiara didn't have hotel reservations for the night of July 21st and likely intended to spend the night at the state park. Monica noted, "The car's mileage shows that she did not veer from the route between the rental car agency and the park. Based on that information, it appears that Khiara intended to take a road trip for one night and then finish up her stay back in Kihei."

It appeared that the key to Khiara's disappearance would likely be found somewhere in Wai'anapanapa State Park. Chris Berquist, who helped coordinate the volunteer search effort, noted that the park was not an easy place to search. "The challenges of working in Hana are not only logistical but also technological. Simply put, there's not much cell coverage out there, so we need to get any apps and maps downloaded beforehand."

Over the next week, police and volunteers combed through Wai'anapanapa State Park looking for any sign of Khiara. A dive team searched the coastal waters while search and rescue personnel scoured the park's lava tubes. A helicopter scanned the area from above. Volunteers used metal detectors to comb the beach on the off chance that Khiara had buried her keys and cell phone in the sand in anticipation of taking a quick swim. They found nothing.

The Hana Community Association, a non-profit organization formed to promote community spirit among those living in the ancient district of Hana, briefly halted the volunteer search so that they could search through the areas of the park that contained sacred sites. Once they cleared the area, the volunteer search recommenced.

Concerned that Khiara may have attempted to leave the park on foot, several search groups scoured the road leading out of the park. On the Facebook page, Chris wrote that they were "trying to cross one more thing off the list, just to make sure she wasn't subject to a hit and run." Once again, searchers came up empty.

The volunteer search was called off on August 4, 2019. Chris Berquist noted, "At this point, we've exhausted our reasonable search area, and we've done everything that we can do unless the police department gives us something else to work with." He was confident that they had done a thorough search, stating that the group had conducted "a coastline search with a helicopter, a dive search of the known caves, and foot searches of the park and its trails" They had also helped distribute missing person flyers throughout the island.

Khiara's family tried to remain optimistic. Monica told a reporter, "We hoped Khiara had a change of mind and went camping or met a fun group of people and went somewhere. She is a spontaneous woman and it would not be unlike her to have a change of plans, but as days go by, we grow more and more worried about her."

Khiara's father, Kevin Henry, made an emotional appeal for help finding his missing daughter. He also had a message for Khiara, telling her that he knew she was an adult and free to go where she wanted, but her family was worried and needed to hear from her. "We just need to know that you're okay. We love you too much not to look for you...we just need to know that you're alive and well."

Investigators obtained surveillance video from both the Aston Maui Mills Resort and the Hertz rental car agency. The footage showed that Khiara was alone when she checked out of the resort as well as when she picked up her rental car. Employees recalled that she had been friendly and appeared relaxed; there was nothing about her behavior that made them think anything was wrong.

The fact that Khiara made hotel reservations for the week following her disappearance and booked a flight home told her parents that she didn't intend to voluntarily disappear. Since extensive searches of Wai'anapanapa State Park failed to yield any evidence of Khiara, they feared that she could have been the victim of foul play.

On September 7, 2019, the family announced that they were offering a $10,000 reward for information leading to Khiara's safe return or to the arrest of the person responsible for her disappearance. Her father made another appeal for help from the public. "We miss her. This has been so hard on us. We just want to know if she's okay. It's been tough…especially not having anything to go on."

The family remained in Maui, hoping for a break in the case. Kevin admitted, "We have nothing to go on. We have no new leads. Every day we're just trying to see where that day takes us." It was hard to not get discouraged.

A few people called to report potential sightings of the missing woman, but none of them could be confirmed. Several people thought they saw her in Hana in the days immediately following her trip to the state park; she was reportedly seen buying something to eat at a food truck and then sitting under a tree reading a book. Unfortunately, none of these sightings were caught on camera so it was impossible to tell if Khiara was the person the witnesses had seen.

Two months after Khiara vanished, her family reluctantly decided to put their search for her on hold. In an update on the "Find Khiara Henry" Facebook page, they wrote, "It's been gut-wrenching not knowing where our daughter is or what may have happened to her. We leave your beautiful island with our heads hung very low." They returned home to California to regroup and decide what their next move should be.

Within a month, the family returned to Hawaii and hired a private investigator to assist in the search for Khiara. On October 25, 2019, they held a rally alongside Hana Highway to remind the public that Khiara was still missing. Thea told a reporter, "Without answers, you don't have closure. We'll never stop looking for her until we get answers and we find her."

Khiara should have been celebrating her 24th birthday on March 7, 2020. Instead, her family marked the day by releasing balloons with notes to Khiara inside them. Monica admitted that the pain of missing Khiara was present every day. "It's been a struggle, a constant battle. We've been having every emotion you could possibly imagine."

As the first anniversary of Khiara's disappearance approached, her family increased the reward they were offering to $15,000. They hoped that the increased amount would bring in some fresh leads, and they praised the Maui community for their constant support over the past year. "When we came to Maui, they embraced us. I want to thank them for keeping an eye out for her and sending tips in."

Although the family was impressed with the assistance they had received from the people of Maui, they were less enamoured with the Maui County Police Department. Khiara's parents decided to establish their own tip line and took the police contact number off of the "Find Khiara Henry" Facebook page because they weren't very responsive when the family called with potential leads. Monica noted, "Our detective does not return our calls."

Despite the passage of time, Monica tried to remain hopeful that Khiara would be found and she pleaded with the public for help. "If anyone knows anything, please say something. Try to keep her in your hearts and minds. She is somebody's daughter and sister. Her whole family would love to have her home."

On August 6, 2021, the Henry family announced that they were increasing the reward for information to $25,000. Her parents and siblings did what they could to keep her disappearance in the public eye, but tips eventually dried up and no new leads were developed. Khiara's case stalled and then went cold.

The investigation was kicked back into high gear on January 13, 2023, when a witness reported seeing a woman she believed was Khiara at a convenience store in Pahoa, Hawaii. Detectives combed through the store's surveillance footage and identified a woman they thought might be Khiara; even the Henry family thought it was possible that Khiara had finally been found.

Investigators staked out the area surrounding the convenience store, hoping the woman would return. A few weeks later, they spotted the woman and interviewed her. Sadly, it wasn't Khiara. Maui Police Detective Sgt. LeeAnn Galario-Guzman told reporters, "[Officers] located a female matching the description of Khiara, however, upon making contact with the female they were able to identify her through her California ID as not being Khiara." It was a devastating blow to the Henry family, but they remain committed to finding Khiara and bringing her home.

Khiara Lavinia Henry was just 23 years old when she vanished while on a solo vacation in Hawaii. An athlete in high school, Khiara loved spending time hiking and was in peak physical condition, but didn't have any wilderness survival training. Khiara has brown eyes and brown hair, and at the time of her disappearance, she was 5 feet 2 inches tall and weighed 105 pounds. She was last seen on surveillance video wearing a black shirt, black pants, black socks, and white sneakers, but these articles were found in her rental car so it's unclear what she was wearing when she disappeared. Khiara has a large tattoo of sunflowers on her upper right arm and a smaller tattoo of praying hands just above her right elbow. If you have any information about Khiara, please contact the Maui County Police Department at 808-244-6400.

Anthony Klama

Anthony Klama – known as Tony to family and friends – liked to play darts. On the evening of Thursday, November 5, 1998, he decided to spend some time doing just that. At 9:00 pm, he left his residence in the Foxfire Apartment complex in Palatine, Illinois, and made the short walk to Splinter's Sports Bar, located just a couple of blocks away. The 36-year-old spent a few hours playing darts there before leaving around 11:45 pm to walk back to his apartment.

Tony had been alone when he left Splinter's Sports Bar, but witnesses would later recall seeing him and an unidentified man get out of a light-colored car in the parking lot of the Foxfire Apartments. The man who was with Tony was described as being around 5 feet 9 inches tall, 190 pounds, with dark hair and a mustache. No one knew who this man was but it was possible it was someone he had been playing darts with while at the sports bar. The two were seen entering the building together, although no one saw where they went once they were inside the building. Tony was never seen again.

Tony was divorced and had no children, but he was extremely close with his family and was in daily contact with his parents and siblings. They grew concerned when they were unable to reach him that Friday; by Saturday, they were certain something was wrong. His car was in the parking lot outside of the apartment building but repeated knocks on his door went unanswered.

Tony worked as a maintenance supervisor at the

Foxfire Apartment complex but none of his coworkers or any of the residents had seen him, so his family called the Palatine Police Department and reported him missing.

Police searched through Tony's apartment and found no signs of foul play. Only one item was unaccounted for: the handset to Tony's cordless phone. A large key ring containing all the master keys for the apartment complex was also missing, but Tony usually kept it clipped to his belt loop so it was possible he had it with him wherever he was.

Investigators obtained Tony's bank records and discovered that he had made two $20 withdrawals on the night he was last seen. Both were made at an ATM located inside Splinter's Sports Bar. There was nothing suspicious about these transactions; Tony had most likely wanted cash so he could pay for his beer at the bar. There was no activity on his bank account after he went missing.

Detectives combed through Tony's phone records and determined that three calls had been made to his apartment in the hours before he was last seen. All three were from payphones; the first one had been made shortly before 9:00 pm from a Shell gas station. It was possible Tony had likely taken this call right before he left to go to Splinter's Sports Bar.

The final two phone calls had come from Dominick's Finer Foods, a grocery store located at 615 E. Dundee Road, about a mile away from Tony's apartment. The calls were made in quick succession around 1:40 am; there was no further phone activity after this.

Although it was unclear who made these phone calls to Tony, the fact that the handset to his cordless phone was missing from his apartment seemed to indicate that the calls were related to his disappearance. He had Caller ID on his phone, so the handset would have displayed all the phone numbers that called him. It was possible those involved in his disappearance were unaware that police would be able to obtain his phone records.

Those closest to Tony knew he would never willingly walk away from his life. He had been excited about a promotion he was expecting to get at work and had never shown any signs of depression; for his family, suicide was not a possibility. They were convinced that foul play was involved in his disappearance, and investigators seemed to agree. Although they found no concrete evidence to suggest that Tony had been harmed, they checked with all area morgues and hospitals in case Tony had been admitted somewhere as a John Doe. They found no one matching Tony's description.

Investigators used search dogs and cadaver dogs to comb through Deer Grove Forest Preserve, located less than four miles from Tony's apartment. It was unclear if they had received any tips pointing them to that location, but they found nothing relevant to the investigation.

According to Tony's family, he wasn't involved in any sort of high-risk activities that might make him a target for murder. He enjoyed drinking beer but never used drugs, and he liked to play darts but wasn't a gambler and didn't owe anyone any money. He had no criminal record and wasn't involved in any illegal activity, nor had he ever mentioned being threatened by anyone. His disappearance was a complete mystery.

Although they were unable to find any evidence pointing to foul play, detectives admitted that there was something strange and unsettling about Tony's disappearance. They were convinced that someone had to know what had happened to Tony and made several public appeals for the person who had called his apartment on the night of his disappearance to come forward. No one did, however, and the investigation soon stalled and went cold.

The Cook County Crime Stoppers program announced that they were offering a $1,000 reward for information leading to Tony's safe return or the arrest and conviction of those responsible for his disappearance, but few tips were received.

Sadly, Tony's case has remained in the cold case files since shortly after he vanished. The last time the case was mentioned by the news media was in 2000. During an interview with a reporter from the Chicago Tribune, Palatine Police Detective Dave Daigle admitted the case was mysterious but declined to provide any further details about the investigation. He was optimistic that it could be solved, noting, "This case is going to break open by someone remembering someone or something." To date, this hasn't happened.

Tony's family refused to give up their search for him and did everything they could to make sure his name remained in the public eye. His older sister, Linda, noted that it was difficult to get publicity for missing adults. Although she stated that the Palatine Police Department had been helpful in her brother's case, as a rule missing adults tended to go unnoticed. "They think if you are over 21, you are free to disappear – especially with males." Hoping to change this, Linda decided to start the Klama Foundation, a non-profit agency dedicated to helping the families of missing adults. The foundation helped countless families before Tony's family decided to disband it.

Anthony Klama was 36 years old when he went missing in 1998. He was very close with his siblings and parents and they do not believe he would have voluntarily left. Tony has green eyes and brown hair, and at the time of his disappearance, he was 6 feet 1 inch tall and weighed around 190 pounds. He was last seen wearing blue jeans, a blue and white flannel shirt, and a blue plaid flannel jacket. He has several Native American-style tattoos on his shoulders and chest. If you have any information about Tony, please contact the Palatine Police Department at 847-359-9000 or the Illinois State Police at 217-785-3327.

Kristi Krebs

When Kristi Krebs left work at 10:00 pm on Monday, August 9, 1993, she told her coworkers that she was going to go straight home. She appeared to be in a cheerful and upbeat mood as she crossed the parking lot of Round Tree Pizza and headed for her red 1990 Toyota Tercel. Coworkers saw her climb into her car and drive out of the parking lot, but the 22-year-old never made it home.

Kristi lived with her parents, Don and Susan Krebs, in Fort Bragg, California. They were worried when their daughter failed to return home from work Monday night, but hoped she might have gone out with some friends. When Kristi still wasn't home the following morning, Bob called the Mendocino County Sheriff's Department and reported her missing.

Deputies spoke with several of Kristi's coworkers at Round Tree Pizza and confirmed that she had left alone the night before. They told investigators that Kristi had seemed to be in an unusually hyper mood during her shift on Monday, but it didn't appear that anything had been bothering her. None of her coworkers were able to provide any clues as to where Kristi might have gone; as far as they knew, she had no plans to do anything other than go home and sleep. She hadn't changed out of her work uniform before leaving the restaurant; when she got into her car she had been wearing blue jeans and a dark blue Round House Pizza shirt.

Although the Mendocino County Sheriff's

Department issued a missing person bulletin with Kristi's information, they had little to go on and there was no formal search for her on Tuesday. With no evidence of foul play, it was assumed that the 22-year-old was missing voluntarily and would soon return home.

All hopes that Kristi would soon come pulling into her driveway were dashed on Tuesday afternoon, when campers in Mendocino Woodlands State Park found her car stuck in a creek bed. There was no sign of Kristi.

It wasn't immediately clear if Kristi herself had driven her car into Mendocino Woodlands State Park or if some type of foul play was involved. Investigators made a public appeal for anyone who had seen Kristi after she left work on Monday night to contact them, and soon received a call from a park ranger at MacKerricher State Park, 20 miles north of Mendocino Woodlands State Park. He was certain he had spoken to Kristi shortly after she was seen leaving Round House Pizza.

According to the park ranger, he had been making his normal patrol through MacKerricher State Park around 10:30 pm Monday night when he saw a red Toyota Tercel sitting in one of the park's parking lots. Since the park had closed at 10:00 pm, the ranger pulled in next to the Toyota to see if anyone was inside. There was only one person in the car, a female seated in the driver's seat. After seeing a picture of Kristi, the ranger identified her as the driver of the car.

Kristi asked the park ranger if it was okay that she was in the parking lot, but he told her that the park was closed and she couldn't remain there overnight. She didn't appear to be upset at this answer and indicated that she would leave. The park ranger noted that the interaction had been a friendly one; nothing seemed to be wrong with Kristi at the time. There was no indication that she was intoxicated or otherwise impaired, and after a few moments she pulled out of the parking lot and left MacKerricher State Park.

Investigators surmised that when Kristi left the parking lot, she drove straight to Mendocino Woodlands State Park. Once there, it appeared she had driven through a remote camping area and ended up on a winding dirt road leading to the Big River creek bed where she got stuck. It was clear that she had made numerous attempts to free her car from the creek bed; detectives determined that she had revved the car's engine so hard that two of the tires had burst. Kristi's car jack was found next to one of her front tires; she had either tried to change the tire or jack the car up in an attempt at getting it unstuck. She had been unsuccessful, and this seemed to make her mad, as it appeared she had repeatedly bashed the car's hood with a rock she found in the creek bed.

Kristi's fit of rage continued when she got back inside the car, where she had taken several photographs out of her wallet and shredded them before tossing the pieces on the front seat. She had also ripped her car stereo out of the dashboard and thrown it onto the seat.

The jeans and shirt Kristi had been wearing when she left work were found in the backseat of her Tercel; although they were neatly folded when found, they were wet, presumably from Kristi's failed attempts at freeing her car. Her gym clothes – a pair of pink Spandex shorts and a white T-shirt with a neon pink and chartreuse design – were missing from the Toyota, leading police to believe that Kristi had changed into them before abandoning her car and setting off on foot.

When Bob and Susan learned that their daughter's car had been found stuck in a creek bed, their thoughts immediately flashed back to an event that had taken place more than three years earlier. In May 1990, Kristi had gotten her car stuck in a wooded location east of Fort Bragg. In a desperate attempt to free her car, she had revved the engine for so long that it had overheated and caught on fire. Panicking and disoriented, Kristi abandoned her car and fled through the woods.

In this earlier incident, Kristi had walked through the night, apparently trying to find her way home. She was found the following morning, confused and disoriented, by a group of men working on some railroad tracks more than 13 miles away from where her car had been left. One of the men was a friend of Kristi's family and recognized her right away; he called her parents and they immediately came to pick her up.

According to Bob, Kristi had seemed to be okay when they started driving home, but a few minutes into the drive it was clear that something was wrong with her. She had no memory of what had happened to her and appeared to be having some sort of mental breakdown. Concerned, her parents drove her directly to a hospital. She spent the next four weeks recovering in a private mental facility, though it would take several months before her memory completely returned.

In the years following this incident, Kristi appeared to be fine and showed no symptoms of mental illness. Her breakdown was attributed to the stress of getting lost in the woods and then having her car catch fire; it seemed to be a singular episode that was unlikely to repeat itself. But in August 1993, more than three years later, it seemed that history was repeating itself.

In hindsight, her father admitted that Kristi had been working herself too hard in the months leading up to her disappearance. She had been holding down two jobs, often working for more than 12 hours a day between

Round House Pizza and Burger King. Although she appeared to be very happy with her life, she began going to the gym more often and sleeping less. Bob now wondered if these were subtle signs that Kristi's mental status was starting to decline. He believed that when Kristi got her car stuck in the woods for a second time, it triggered a flashback of the first incident. "I think it was just too much for her."

The Mendocino County Sheriff's Department, along with volunteers and search dogs, launched an intensive search of Mendocino Woods State Park and the area surrounding where Kristi's car had been found. Nothing was found to indicate that foul play was involved in her disappearance and detectives believed that she had walked away from her car voluntarily, though it was unclear what her state of mind was at the time. Her parents believed that she was likely disoriented and possibly suffering from memory loss.

The search of Mendocino Woodlands State Park continued throughout the week. Search parties combed along all the main roads leading in and out of the park, while the Mendocino County Air Squadron conducted an aerial search of the numerous logging trails that snaked through the thick woodlands. All searches came up empty.

On Monday, a week after Kristi went missing, the Mendocino County Sheriff's Department announced that their search of Mendocino Woodlands State Park was being called off. The ground and aerial searches had covered more than 1800 square miles but failed to find any trace of Kristi. Mendocino County Lt. Rich Wiseman noted that they had thoroughly covered the area but found nothing to indicate that Kristi was still inside the state park. "Without further information, we just don't think we can do anything else."

Although the search of the park failed to yield any clues, several people called detectives to report seeing Kristi in the days following her disappearance. One man was certain he had seen the missing woman hitchhiking on Highway 20 near Fort Bragg. "There were a number of people standing there hitchhiking near the road that goes up to Harvest Market and she was with them." The man thought at first that the young woman was his niece, so he slowed down as he approached the group of hitchhikers and got a good look at the woman he believed was Kristi.

The sighting had taken place on August 10th, the day after Kristi went missing. The man was able to accurately describe the hot pink shorts the woman was wearing, and Susan was confident that the man had seen her daughter. Unfortunately, by the time investigators followed up on the reported sighting, the hitchhikers were no longer in the area.

Kristi's parents were hopeful that their daughter would be located quickly, but as days and then weeks went by without any progress on the case they struggled to remain optimistic. Bob told reporters, "We feel our daughter is out there and doesn't know who she is. With the help of the public, we hope to get her back."

By December, Kristi had been missing for four months. Bob and Susan faced the grim task of getting through the holiday season without their daughter, and concentrated on keeping her story in the public eye. Noting that Kristi could be just about anywhere by that point, they expanded their search outside of California into several other western states.

Members of the Fort Bragg community started a fund so they could help cover the costs of the continued search for Kristi and offer a reward for her return. By March 1994, they had collected more than $40,000.

Despite the monetary reward being offered, tips about Kristi's possible whereabouts slowed to a trickle.

Nine months after Kristi vanished, a woman saw her missing poster in a Salt Lake City, Utah, gas station and recognized her as a hitchhiker she had picked up the previous August. Alicia Larson immediately called the tip line and reported that she was certain she had picked Kristi up in Salt Lake City a few days after she was last seen in California. She was so certain that the hitchhiker had been Kristi that when she didn't get a call back from detectives she decided to call Kristi's parents.

Alicia told Bob and Susan that she had encountered Kristi near Interstate 80 in Salt Lake City on August 11th, two days after she was last seen in California. She accurately described the hot pink shorts and distinctive t-shirt that Kristi had been wearing, and noted that the hitchhiker had introduced herself as Kris. As she got into Alicia's car, she stated, "You're looking at the happiest girl in the world," a phrase Susan confirmed was one that her daughter used often.

Alicia stated that Kristi had been happy and talkative, claiming that she was in love with a truck driver and was traveling to Amarillo, Texas, to marry him. As Kristi continued talking, however, Alicia sensed that something wasn't quite right with her. When the young woman confided that she was being chased by police and couldn't go home because it would put her family in danger, Alicia realized that "the story she was telling me wasn't real. It was clear very quickly to me that she was in a world of her own."

Alicia eventually dropped the hitchhiker off at a McDonald's in Park City, Utah. As the young woman got out of the car, she remarked, "Burger King is better." Since Kristi worked at Burger King at the time of her disappearance, her parents confirmed that this was also something Kristi likely would have said.

Kristi's parents were convinced that Alicia had indeed picked up their daughter. Susan noted, "She told us about conversations and mannerisms that were completely credible, that anyone who knew Kristi would recognize...we know she hitchhiked out of Fort Bragg and made it to Salt Lake City in a very happy, though delusional, state." After that, her trail went cold.

In an effort to increase publicity about the case and hopefully solicit some viable leads, Kristi's disappearance was featured on an episode of America's Most Wanted in May 1994. The broadcast brought in many reported sightings but none of them could be confirmed.

In February 1995, a 12-minute segment on Kristi's case was featured on Unsolved Mysteries and watched by more than 20 million people. Again, a flood of new tips came in but none of them led to Kristi.

Over time, Kristi's case faded from the headlines. Although her parents have never stopped hoping that Kristi will be found alive, police are less optimistic. Despite the numerous reported sightings, some investigators admit that they have never been able to confirm that Kristi actually left the Fort Bragg area and they are unsure if she is still alive.

In 2012, Fort Bragg Police Officer Jeanine Gregory requested that the National Center for Missing and Exploited Children produce an age-progression photo of Kristi to show what she might look like as a 40-year-old woman. Officer Gregory was convinced the case could still be solved. "I'm optimistic that either she's out there somewhere or someone knows something about it."

Kristi Krebs was 22 years old when she went

missing in 1993. She has blue eyes and brown hair, and at the time of her disappearance, she was 5 feet 2 inches tall and weighed 140 pounds. She was last seen wearing pink gym shorts and a t-shirt with a neon pink, chartreuse, and blue design. Her right thumb is deformed and thick at the knuckle and she speaks with a slight lisp. She was most likely suffering from some psychological trauma at the time of her disappearance and may have issues with her memory. If you have any information about Kristi, please contact the Fort Bragg Police Department at 707-961-2820.

Steven MacKrell

Steven MacKrell was in a great mood on the evening of Wednesday, July 29, 2015. The 25-year-old spent much of the evening with friends and a few family members at Lucky's Tavern, a popular bar in downtown Fort Lauderdale, Florida. Around 1:30 am, Steven and several friends left the bar but weren't ready for the night to end. Although they each went separate ways to retrieve their respective cars, they agreed to meet up in the parking lot of a nearby Walgreens to plan their next move. Steven never arrived at Walgreens and his friends would never see him again.

Steven lived with his parents, Donald and Astrid MacKrell, in Fort Lauderdale and worked as a professional poker dealer at Gulfstream Park in Hallandale Beach, Florida. His parents started to grow concerned when they didn't hear from him at all on Thursday, but when he failed to show up for work on Friday they knew that something was wrong. Astrid called the Fort Lauderdale Police Department and reported her son missing.

Steven was the youngest of Donald and Astrid's three sons and was very close with his brothers, Michael and Kevin. Michael had been at Lucky's Tavern with Steven on Wednesday night, but he had to work in the morning so had left around 11:00 pm. Michael knew that Steven had several drinks while he was at the bar and had told him to be careful. "Before I left, I told him that I loved him and to just go home." Steven hadn't heeded his warning.

When Steven left Lucky's Tavern, he returned to his

car, which was parked on West Los Olas Boulevard in downtown Fort Lauderdale. He was seen driving north on Northwest Seventh Avenue, presumably heading toward the Walgreens where he had agreed to meet his friends. It was only a short distance away, at the corner of Broward Boulevard and Seventh Avenue. His friends waited for him but he never showed up.

Detectives noted that there were a number of surveillance cameras in the area where Steven was last seen, but it would take several days before they could gather all of the relevant footage. While they waited, they started interviewing everyone who had been with Steven in the hours leading up to his disappearance.

Investigators learned that Steven had worked an overnight shift at the casino Tuesday, then left at 4:00 am and went on a 13-hour fishing trip with his cousin, Sam Navarete. Steven managed to nap for a while on the boat, and once they got back to shore he was ready for a night out on the town. After grabbing a quick shower at Sam's house, Steven and his cousin headed straight for Lucky's Tavern.

While Steven was at the bar, his cell phone battery died and he didn't have his charger with him. This meant he would have been unable to call for help if he ran into trouble; it also made it impossible for detectives to use phone pings to determine Steven's location. Phone records showed that the phone was never turned back on after its battery died that night.

Aware of the fact that Steven had been drinking, detectives thought it was possible he had been in a car accident. They scoured along all the possible routes Steven might have taken but found no sign of him or his white Ford Fusion. Concerned that he could have crashed his car into one of the many waterways in the area, the Fort

Lauderdale Nautical Unit conducted several sonar searches but failed to find anything.

Steven's family was certain he wouldn't have disappeared voluntarily; he was the father of a 1-year-old daughter and he absolutely adored her. He had also been talking about getting married to his longtime girlfriend. Those who knew him well told investigators that there was no way Steven would have walked away from his life.

Friends and family members spent the weekend hanging up missing person posters throughout the downtown Fort Lauderdale area. Kevin told reporters that he was worried about his younger brother. "It's like he vanished into thin air. He hasn't touched his debit card and hasn't shown up for work, and he never misses work."

Kevin admitted that Steven's sudden disappearance was baffling to his family. "It's so out of the ordinary for him, he never misses work and would never just take off without contacting anyone, that's just not him." Steven, who had been born at Plantation General Hospital in Fort Lauderdale, had spent his entire life in the area and had "never been away from South Florida." He simply wasn't the kind of person who would take an impromptu trip without letting someone know.

As days went by without any word from Steven, his loved ones grew even more worried. Kevin noted, "We're so close as a family. He's more than a brother, he's my best friend. My mother is having a really hard time. I'm just trying to hold it together...you can't imagine what the family is going through right now." It was especially hard for his daughter, who had celebrated her first birthday just a few weeks before Steven vanished. She missed her father and didn't understand why she couldn't see him.

Nearly two weeks after Steven was last seen, investigators discovered that he had used one of his credit cards at a Pompano Beach gas station about an hour after he left the Lucky Tavern in Fort Lauderdale. It was the first potential break in the case, though no one knew why Steven would have made the 15-mile drive to Pompano Beach that night.

Detectives obtained surveillance footage of Steven from inside the Valero gas station on North Dixie Highway. It showed the missing man enter the store at 2:32 am and head for the snack aisle of the small store. Steven was stumbling slightly as he walked and appeared to be somewhat intoxicated, but not enough that it raised any red flags with the store clerk. He spent a few minutes contemplating different snack options, then walked to the counter where he used his credit card to pay for the $6.00 bill. He spent a few minutes chatting with two young women who were inside the gas station before he finally walked out into the parking lot.

After viewing the footage, Kevin noted, "There's no doubt that's him on the video." He was somewhat comforted to learn that Steven had made it out of Fort Lauderdale that night. "There's a lot of sketchy things that go on downtown in the late night hours, so I'm a bit relieved to get him out of that area, but it still doesn't answer any questions for us."

The following week, investigators announced that they had obtained additional surveillance video of Steven from outside the Valero gas station; this footage would change the course of the investigation. It showed Steven standing next to his Ford Fusion, which was parked at one of the gas pumps. He was talking to the occupants of a small silver car, perhaps a Chevrolet Malibu or Impala. Steven could be seen leaning in the driver's side window of the silver car, which was pulled up alongside his car. There was no sound on the video, so it's unclear what

Steven was saying, but he appeared to be upset.

As the silver car started to pull away, Steven stepped back and appeared to throw his drink at the vehicle. The silver car left the gas station, but circled back and pulled up next to the gas pump immediately behind Steven's car. Steven can then be seen driving away from the pump and pulling out of the parking lot with the silver car speeding after him.

After watching the footage, Kevin noted, "At this point, this is our strongest lead. Whoever followed my brother out of that gas station – whoever chased him – has to know something. Detectives obtained surveillance footage of the silver car's passenger as he went inside to buy something; they released a picture of this man and asked for help from the public in identifying him.

Fort Lauderdale Police Detective Kevin Dupree told reporters that they had no evidence suggesting that the occupants of the silver car had any involvement in Steven's disappearance, but investigators wanted to speak with them to see if they could provide any additional information about where Steven went when he left the gas station.

Steven's family wasn't so sure about the people in the silver car; Astrid feared that they had chased after Steven with ill intentions in mind. She thought it was possible that they had caught up with him and murdered him, but tried to remain optimistic. Kevin made a plea to the public for help. "If you know something, can you please step up and say something? This man has a family back at home who's worried about him and a new baby who wants to know her father."

A month after Steven was last seen, it appeared that the investigation had started to stall. There had been no reported sightings of Steven and the identity of the occupants of the silver car remained unknown. Hoping to generate some new tips, Broward Crimestoppers announced that they were offering a $3,000 reward for information leading to the arrest of anyone responsible for Steven's disappearance.

In October, Steven's family along with members of the Fort Lauderdale Police Department held a press conference to raise awareness about the case. It was clear that going months without any answers was starting to have a toll on Steven's loved ones. Astrid told reporters, "This is something that no parent should go through. The not knowing what happened, the not knowing where he's at...it's a really painful moment that this family is going through." Steven's father, Donald, agreed. "Every day that goes by is one day longer without any answers."

Investigators appealed to the public for help in finding Steven. Detective Tracy Figone stressed that no tip was too small to be called in. "Anything at this point would help. Anything that you might not think is a big deal, let the police decide. It may end up being one of the biggest leads we've had this far."

Months went by and there was no movement on the case. The Fort Lauderdale Police Department, the Broward County Sheriff's Office, and the volunteer group Guardians for the Missing joined forces to search through countless waterways in both Fort Lauderdale and Pompano Beach. They found dozens of cars, but Steven's Ford Fusion remained missing.

Astrid organized a prayer service to mark the first anniversary of Steven's disappearance. "It's not a vigil because we are holding onto hope that he is still alive." She made another plea for anyone who knew anything about what had happened to her son to call police. "We're going crazy trying to figure this out. We need people to step forward with information about what happened to Steven."

Detectives admitted that they still had no idea what had happened after Steven pulled away from the Pompano Beach Valero station. His license plate was never scanned by any license plate readers, indicating that he hadn't left the area. They used helicopters, boats equipped with sonar, and divers to comb through dozens of canals and waterways that Steven might have driven past. Each search failed to yield any clues to Steven's fate.

In February 2017, Steven's family announced that they were offering a $7,000 reward for information leading to Steven's whereabouts. This was in addition to the $3,000 reward being offered by Crimestoppers, bringing the total available reward to $10,000. They were hopeful that the additional money would bring in new tips, but the money went unclaimed.

Alison McManus, founder of Guardians for the Missing, joined the search for Steven shortly after he went missing. Her group, which uses sonar to locate vehicles underwater, has spent countless hours scanning different waterways looking for Steven's missing Ford Fusion. "Anywhere we can find that he might have went or driven, we have searched." They were able to locate dozens of vehicles, many of which had been stolen, but have been unable to locate Steven's car.

In April 2022, the group Adventures with Purpose spent two days searching through different bodies of water in Fort Lauderdale and Pompano Beach in search of Steven and his vehicle. They found several cars, including one that had six bullet holes in its driver's side door, but found nothing related to Steven.

As of March 2023, Steven remains missing. Detectives admit that they have no idea what happened to him and are keeping all options open. They do not believe that he chose to voluntarily disappear, but are unsure if he met with foul play or was simply involved in a tragic accident. The identities of the occupants of the silver car seen following Steven remain unknown; although they are not considered suspects in his disappearance, they may hold the key to locating Steven.

Steven James MacKrell was 25 years old when he went missing from Pompano Beach, Florida in July 2015. He was last seen on surveillance camera being followed by a small silver sedan, and it's unclear if the occupants of this car were involved in his disappearance. Steven has brown eyes and brown hair, and at the time of his disappearance, he was 5 feet 10 inches tall and weighed 165 pounds. He was last seen wearing a gray T-shirt, khaki pants, and black shoes. His car, a white four-door Ford Fusion with Florida license plate WJ70L, is also missing. If you have any information about Steven, please contact the Fort Lauderdale Police Department at 954-828-5700.

Amos Mortier

Amos Mortier got home from class around 1:00 pm on the afternoon of Monday, November 8, 2004. He parked his car in the driveway of his rented home in Fitchburg, Wisconsin, and went inside to greet his husky mix, Gnosis. He made a phone call to a friend at 1:20 pm, then put a Jurassic 5 album on his turntable. At some point after that, the 27-year-old vanished without a trace.

Amos was a student at Madison Area Technical College in Madison, Wisconsin; he was studying ecology and botany in the hopes of becoming an organic farmer. Although he hadn't been very enthusiastic about academics when he was in high school, he was happy with his decision to go back to school and doing well in all his classes.

Jesse Settle was one of the last people known to see Amos. He had run into him on MATC's campus around 11:30 am on Monday. "I thought he was going to play some pinball between classes in the lounge." At some point, however, Amos left the campus and never returned. Jesse was somewhat surprised when Amos didn't attend any of his other classes that week, but he wasn't overly concerned. He assumed that something had come up and Amos would eventually be back with a good explanation for where he had been.

Amos was supposed to meet up with some of his friends for dinner on Tuesday night but failed to show up. They left several voicemails on his cell phone but didn't hear back from him. After a few more days went by without any word from Amos, they started to get worried. Several friends drove to his house that Saturday; they knocked on the front door but got no answer.

Both of Amos's vehicles were parked in the driveway and his friends noticed that his bookbag was inside one of his cars. Worried that he might have hurt himself, they decided to break into his house. The front door was locked, but they noticed that the door leading from the garage into the house was open. Cautiously, they went inside, calling out for their friend.

The house was dark but not quiet. Curiously, two turntables were still spinning; it appeared Amos had been listening to music and then was suddenly called away. The record had long since reached the end and was emitting a staticky sound as it spun endlessly around. There was no sign of Amos or his dog.

Amos's friends were confused; his wallet and a $1,000 check his grandmother had sent him to help pay for his tuition were lying on a table, and the fact that both of his cars were parked outside indicated that Amos couldn't have gone far on his own. They decided it would be best to contact some of Amos's family members to see if they knew where the missing man could be. They used the contact information listed on the check written by his grandmother to find out the phone number for his mom, Margie Milutinovich.

One of Amos's friends called Margie at 9:30 pm Sunday and asked if she had spoken with her son. Margie was surprised to learn that no one had seen Amos for nearly a week; she immediately knew that something had to be wrong. At 6:30 am the following morning, she called the Fitchburg Police Department and reported Amos missing.

Officers were dispatched to Amos's rented home to

conduct a welfare check. They arrived at 6:40 am and found no sign of Amos. Although they didn't find anything inside the home to suggest that foul play had taken place, they were concerned by the length of time he had been missing and immediately launched a search of the surrounding area.

Amos had moved into the rental home, which sat on 2.3 acres of land, on August 1, 2004; he was still in the process of hanging pictures and decorating the house when he disappeared. He kept to himself; his closest neighbors told police that they had never met him. As police canvassed the neighborhood, they learned that one of Amos's neighbors had found Gnosis running loose without a collar shortly after Amos was last seen. Not knowing who the dog belonged to, the neighbor had allowed the dog to stay at her home. Amos's family members were thrilled to reunite with Gnosis, but it didn't bring them any closer to finding Amos.

Initially, police thought it was possible that Amos had taken Gnosis for a walk in the woods and somehow gotten injured, preventing him from getting home. If he had been injured, finding him quickly was imperative; he had already been missing for a week. They combed through the woods, cornfields, and marshland that surrounded his property but didn't find any sign of him.

The search effort intensified on Tuesday. Police officers and firefighters were joined by some of Amos's friends and family members as they combed through the rural area surrounding Amos's home. The Dane County Sheriff's Office set up a mobile command center in a parking lot on Lacy Road; the Badger Chapter of the American Red Cross set up a refreshment station in Amos's driveway, providing hot drinks, sandwiches, and snacks to the searchers.

By Wednesday, more of Amos's friends and classmates had learned that he was missing and showed up to help in the search. Fitchburg Police Lt. Jay Wilson told reporters that it was very unusual for Amos to be out of contact with people for an extended period of time, leading police to worry for his welfare. "We've got a lot of resources that we've gathered to try and locate this gentleman." Despite their efforts, they found no clues to Amos's whereabouts.

By Friday, the physical search for Amos was winding down. Fields, marshes, and wooded areas within a one-mile radius of Amos's home had been searched, as had several properties within the same radius. Nothing had been found.

The ground search was called off on Saturday. Fitchburg Police Sgt. Don Bomkamp noted that deer hunting season was scheduled to start that day, meaning that armed hunters would be roaming the woodlands. Officials were unwilling to risk the safety of any of the searchers, so discontinued the volunteer search. Police officers continued looking for Amos, however, and spent Saturday scouring several small bodies of water for any sign of the missing man. They came up empty.

Although detectives were unable to rule out the possibility that Amos had voluntarily disappeared, they didn't believe it was likely. Deputy Chief Don Bates referred to the disappearance as suspicious, noting, "It's frustrating. We are concerned." He admitted that it was very out of character for Amos to be out of contact with his family, leading investigators to fear that foul play may have been involved.

Detectives learned that Amos owned some property in Grant County, where he had a trailer and a large garden. A team was sent to search that area but found nothing to indicate that Amos had been there recently.

Amos had spent some time volunteering with an urban agricultural project in Milwaukee, leading investigators to expand their search into the city. Hoping to reach as many people as possible, they reached out to the local news media to help spread the word. They asked anyone who knew Amos to contact detectives.

Weeks went by with little progress on the case. A month after Amos was last seen, Lt. Jay Wilson admitted that he thought Amos had fallen victim to foul play. He noted that Amos never would have willingly left his dog unattended, and investigators had been unable to find any other logical explanation for his disappearance.

Margie refused to believe that her son could be dead. She was convinced that he was still alive somewhere but was suffering from amnesia and unable to find his way home. She and Amos's friends turned to the internet to raise awareness about his disappearance. They created a website, www.findamos.com, that included information about the case, downloadable flyers, and pictures of the missing man. Anyone who thought they knew anything was encouraged to get in contact with Margie so she could follow up with them.

Hoping that increased publicity would bring in more tips about Amos's whereabouts, Adams Outdoor Advertising company donated a billboard for the family to use. The billboard, located in a prominent place on the eastbound Beltway, featured pictures of Amos and a phone number that people could call with any tips.

On December 8th, police used a search dog to comb through a landfill located on Highway MM near McCoy Road in Fitchburg. The landfill was near Amos's home, but it wasn't clear if detectives were following up on a specific tip or simply trying to eliminate the possibility that Amos's body had been left there. They didn't find anything, but Lt. Wilson told reporters that they weren't giving up on the case. "We have a team of people and are working every day to return him to his family."

Friends described Amos as a private person who had a great sense of humor and cared deeply for the environment. Miranda Maysack noted, "He's able to jump into any conversation and make witty remarks about anything." Amos had a close relationship with his mother and was devoted to his dog, Gnosis. He hoped to eventually move to North Carolina and pursue his dream of organic farming; it was something he was very passionate about and he had enjoyed teaching children in Milwaukee how they could grow their own vegetables in rooftop gardens. None of his friends believed he would have simply walked away from his life without saying a word to anyone.

As weeks went by, Margie grew increasingly desperate to find her son. She worried that he had been in some kind of accident in the woods, telling a reporter that she couldn't help but wonder if he was lying injured at the bottom of a forgotten well somewhere in the remote Wisconsin woodland. "You don't want to sleep, you don't want to eat, you don't want to be comfortable if your son could be hurt and cold."

By the middle of December, Margie was growing increasingly frustrated with the situation. She was angry because she believed some of Amos's friends had more information than they were sharing with police and frustrated because police refused to share information about the case with her. She just wanted answers.

Margie admitted that Amos had been involved with drugs in his past; in 1996 he had been arrested after selling psilocybin mushrooms to an undercover law enforcement officer. He had eventually pleaded guilty to a misdemeanor charge of possession. According to Margie, Amos had decided to clean his life up after that. "He quit everything and he really cleaned himself up. He was at a peak when he became missing."

Margie was consumed by searching for her son. As the Christmas season approached, she had no plans to celebrate. "I'll be in front of my computer, researching and trying to find any clues that I can."

Behind the scenes, detectives were still doing everything they could to locate Amos. By the end of the year, it was clear that they believed that Amos had still been dealing in illicit drugs and that this had something to do with his disappearance. Unlike Margie, they didn't seem to believe that Amos was still alive. They launched a John Doe investigation – similar to a grand jury investigation but conducted by a magistrate instead of a jury – to determine if there was any criminal wrongdoing involved in his disappearance. Detectives admitted that they were having a hard time getting some of Amos's friends to speak with them; this proceeding was a way of getting information from them.

Both Dane County Sheriff's Detective David Bongiovani and Fitchburg Detective Shannan Sheil-Morgan had been assigned solely to Amos's case since he was reported missing; they had interviewed nearly 100 people but still had no solid evidence pointing to what had happened to him. Although they assured the public that they weren't limiting their investigation to a possible drug connection, it appeared that they were leaning in that direction.

In April 2005, Amos's family announced that they were offering a $10,000 reward for information leading to his whereabouts. Around the same time, detectives announced that they believed Amos had been the victim of a drug-related murder. Fitchburg Deputy Police Chief Don Bates told reporters, "It is apparent that Amos's disappearance is related to his drug activity and proceeds thereof." He didn't go into any further details about what sort of drugs Amos was allegedly involved with and admitted that they had no evidence proving that Amos had been murdered.

Margie disputed the police conclusion that Amos had been involved with drugs and told reporters that she was still holding on to the hope that he was alive somewhere. Her hopes were bolstered in June 2005, when three different nurses came forward to report treating a man they believed had been Amos. He had been an attendee at the Bonnaroo music festival in Tennessee at the time and had reported having problems with his memory; he had some facial injuries and stated that he didn't know his name.

Investigators followed up on the tip by forwarding Amos's picture to every sheriff's office in Tennessee; detectives were sent to check around the festival campgrounds but didn't find anyone matching Amos's description. They also asked for people who had taken pictures at the festival to send them copies so they could look through them, but they found no evidence that Amos had been at the event.

Once it became clear that police were focusing on drugs as the catalyst for Amos's disappearance, a rift formed between law enforcement and Margie. When friends and family held a "gathering of hope" to mark the first anniversary of the disappearance, Margie made it clear that police were not welcome. "None of the information the police have released has been substantiated, therefore, the family and friends of Amos have no choice but to disbelieve any information the police have regarding this case."

There were allegations that Amos had been dealing marijuana to pay his bills; detectives noted that he was paying rent in Dane County and a mortgage in Grant County but didn't appear to have a steady job while he was going to school. He associated with people who were known to be involved in the drug trade, and his friends later admitted that they had removed marijuana from his home prior to calling the police to report him missing because they didn't want him to get into trouble.

In July 2007, court records pertaining to the John Doe investigation were unsealed. According to testimony provided by some of Amos's friends, he was owed a great deal of money by someone for marijuana he had provided and he intended to confront this person shortly before he went missing. One friend claimed Amos was owed as much as $90,000; Amos claimed he wanted to confront this person but was afraid of them.

Margie was pleased that the court records were unsealed but didn't believe that they contained the correct information regarding her son's disappearance. She believed that some of Amos's friends had been lying to protect themselves from prosecution; indeed, several of them would later be convicted of various drug charges and sent to prison. It was unclear who to believe.

During the course of the investigation, police conducted a total of 18 searches. Amos's home, trailer, cars, storage locker, and the homes of two friends were among the properties that were searched. Investigators found spots of what they believed to be blood in a bathroom in Amos's house but no definitive signs of foul play. Dane County District Attorney Brian Blanchard told reporters that no charges were imminent in the case. "We do not have evidence justifying bringing criminal charges against anyone in connection with [Amos's] disappearance."

The case soon faded from the headlines, though Margie refused to give up the search for her son. As years have passed, it has become more difficult to know who to believe regarding what happened in the days leading up to Amos's disappearance. The fact that he was dealing marijuana is undeniable; whether or not it led to his vanishing is still up for debate.

Although some friends testified that Amos was owed a substantial sum of money from someone, others claimed that it was Amos himself who owed money. Others believe that Amos may have learned that his marijuana operations were under investigation and decided that he was going to go into hiding. Those who knew him best, however, refuse to believe that he ever would have left his beloved Gnosis behind.

The fact that Gnosis was found running loose by a neighbor could indicate that Amos was indeed out for a walk with him when something happened. The area surrounding his home contained vast cornfields, densely wooded areas, and marshland. It's very possible that he did have some kind of accident and was unable to get to safety before succumbing to the elements. Until his body is found or someone confesses to killing him, the truth may never be known.

Amos Mortier was 27 years old when he went missing in 2004. He was a gentle and witty young man who loved the outdoors and was devoted to his dog, Gnosis. The circumstances surrounding his disappearance are murky and there are many possibilities about what might have happened to him. His mother, Margie, has never stopped searching for him and continues to hope that he will be found. Amos has hazel eyes and brown hair, and at the time of his disappearance, he was 5 feet 5 inches tall and weighed 130 pounds. His top teeth are crooked and he has a scar above his right eyebrow. When last seen, Amos was wearing a hooded brown Carhartt jacket, blue jeans, and brown hiking boots. If you have any information about Amos, please contact the Fitchburg Police Department at 608-270-4300.

Laura Nimbach

Laura Nimbach had been going through a rough patch in life at the beginning of 2009, but she was taking steps to turn things around and was optimistic about the future. The 22-year-old had been staying in a domestic violence shelter after leaving her abusive boyfriend but checked out of it on February 16, 2009, for reasons that are unclear.

A deputy with the Pinellas County Sheriff's Office found Laura sleeping behind a building on 49th Street in St. Petersburg, Florida on the evening of Tuesday, February 17, 2009. The deputy woke her up and recommended that she check into one of the homeless shelters in the area. After speaking with the deputy for a few minutes, Laura left the area where she had been sleeping but never checked into any local shelters and was never seen again.

At the time of her disappearance, Laura had been living in Florida for about three years. She was born and raised in Livonia, Michigan; she initially lived with her mother and two older sisters. Her mother had some mental health issues, and when Laura was 5 years old her father gained custody of her.

Laura learned to be self-sufficient at an early age. Her father had a gambling addiction and seldom had money to spare. Determined to attend a private Catholic high school, Laura worked as a nanny in order to pay for her own tuition. She was an excellent student, maintaining high grades while participating in volleyball, soccer, and softball. Her sister Rene noted, "She was the golden child."

After she graduated from high school, Laura enrolled in the nursing program at Wayne State University, working nights at a bar in order to pay for the program. She spent two years at Wayne State, but eventually the pressure of trying to both work and go to school full-time became too much for her and she ended up dropping out.

In 2006, Laura decided to leave Michigan. She was in an abusive relationship with a man named Nick and was ready to make a fresh start somewhere new. She moved to Clearwater, Florida, where her high school best friend, Amanda Botts, was living with a roommate. Laura soon found a job at a local restaurant and started taking classes to become an ultrasound technician. She bought herself a new car and rented a nice apartment on the beach. To her sisters, she seemed to be living a dream life in Florida. Amanda eventually moved back to Michigan, but Laura loved living in Florida and decided to stay there.

At some point, Laura started dating a man named Sean Wheeler. He had been arrested several times in the past for various weapons and drug charges, and he was very abusive toward Laura. Despite his propensity for violence, Laura was drawn to Sean and seemed unable to break free from him.

Laura was in a car accident in 2007 and prescribed oxycodone to help manage her pain. Although she had never had any drug problems in the past, she soon found herself addicted to oxycodone. She later told her sister, Marilyn, that the addiction was something she never saw coming. "She switched from using what the doctors gave her to drug dealers…one day she was taking pain pills, then she was snorting them." Although Laura realized that she had a problem, she tried to hide it from her friends and family whenever she spoke to them on the phone. They had no idea that Laura's life was beginning to spiral out of control.

Sean was a known drug dealer and made sure Laura always had a steady supply of the drug. Like many users, Laura became a different person when she was under the influence. Amanda could tell that something was wrong; she described Laura as being erratic, violent, and very aggressive when she was high. She tried to convince her to get help, but Laura seemed unable to break the hold that oxycodone had on her.

Laura hit rock bottom in November 2008. She and Sean got into a violent argument that spilled outside; police were called after a witness saw Sean repeatedly slamming Laura's head on the sidewalk. Sean was arrested and charged with battery.

Shortly after Sean beat her, Laura found the duffel bag where he kept his drug supply and took a bottle of oxycodone out of it. Tired of dealing with everything, she swallowed 250 tablets in an apparent suicide attempt. She was taken to the hospital where she remained in a coma for a few days; doctors determined that the overdose had caused organ failure. Her sisters, Rene and Marilyn, flew to Florida to be by her side.

For Laura's loved ones, her descent into drug addiction and resulting suicide attempt had been completely unexpected. As Marilyn later recalled, "This all happened very fast. We had a normal sister that was going to college and had her stuff together, and then the next thing we knew, this literally happened within a year...we were just stunned."

Miraculously, Laura survived her suicide attempt and was released from the hospital, though she was warned that she would likely suffer some lingering effects from heart and kidney damage. Her sisters were determined to help her get her life back on track. They helped her pack all her belongings and arranged for her to enter a drug rehabilitation facility in Kentucky, where their mother lived. Laura was ready to get clean; over the next month, she managed to break free from her addiction and was determined to remain sober.

When Laura returned to Florida in late January 2009, she didn't plan on staying there indefinitely. She had to appear in court on a charge she had picked up while she was on drugs; she also planned to testify against Sean in his upcoming battery trial that was scheduled for February 18, 2009. She vanished the night before he went on trial.

It didn't take long for Laura's loved ones to realize that something was wrong. When she returned to Florida, Laura didn't have a permanent place to stay so she bounced between a cousin's house, friends' couches, and women's shelters. No matter where she stayed, she made sure that she was in constant contact with her sisters and mother. According to Marilyn, "We talked every day and she was staying sober…she was doing well." Then, without warning, she stopped calling.

Rene, Marilyn, and Amanda all tried reaching Laura on her cell phone, but within a couple of days her voicemail was full and it was clear she hadn't checked any of her messages. Concerned, they started calling hospitals and shelters throughout Pinellas County, but none of them had any record of Laura.

By the end of the week, Rene was convinced that something was wrong. "It went from us talking to her on a daily basis to nothing at all." From Colorado, she and Marilyn struggled to get Florida law enforcement to take Laura's disappearance seriously. "We got nowhere…they refused to look for her and they refused to take a missing person report."

Officials at the Pinellas County Sheriff's Office had a

multitude of reasons – or excuses – for why they didn't consider Laura to be a missing person. They told Rene and Marilyn that Laura was an adult, free to go missing if she wanted. She had battled a drug problem in the past and might have disappeared to avoid going to court. They also implied that Laura wasn't really a resident of Florida at the time she went missing – they considered her to be a homeless transient. It took six weeks – and a phone call to the FBI – before Pinellas County finally agreed to accept a missing person report.

It was a frustrating time for Laura's loved ones. Marilyn noted, "Laura wasn't just some drug addict on the street, Laura had a whole life...she was close to her family." Both Rene and Marilyn did everything they could to gain publicity for Laura's disappearance, but they were living in Colorado and the distance was a problem.

Amanda, who was living in Michigan, decided to use the power of the internet to spread awareness about her missing best friend. She created Myspace and Facebook pages about Laura's disappearance and soon built a small network of local volunteers who distributed missing person flyers throughout Pinellas County.

Melissa Hutcheon was one of the volunteers assisting in the search for Laura. She didn't know Laura personally, but they had some mutual friends and when she learned she was missing she was quick to offer her help. "So many people are hurting and you can't do anything, but in this case, I can do something." She, along with dozens of other locals, spent hours visiting gas stations, coffee shops, and markets, hanging up missing posters and looking for anyone who might have information about Laura.

As word about Laura's disappearance spread, her family started receiving tips about possible sightings of the missing woman. They passed each tip on to the Pinellas County Sheriff's Office, but they didn't believe that police followed up on any of their reports.

From the beginning, Laura's loved ones thought that Sean Wheeler was possibly involved in her disappearance. The timing was certainly suspicious; Laura went missing immediately before she was due in court to testify against Sean. They told law enforcement about their suspicions, but deputies appeared to brush them off, insisting that Sean had no involvement in Laura's disappearance.

It doesn't appear that the Pinellas County Sheriff's Office made any real attempt at finding Laura. Her family believes that they wrote Laura off as "just another drug addict" who had vanished to avoid having to testify in court. Marilyn noted, "Detectives never call us...I don't think I've gotten a call from a detective in years. Even when she first went missing, they didn't really seem to care."

The fact that six weeks went by before police would agree to take a missing person report is certainly a tragedy; if Laura did meet with foul play, her killer had ample time to get rid of any evidence.

Laura has now been missing for more than 14 years, and her family knows no more than they did on the day they first realized she was missing. Rene continues to hope for the best. "We don't give up hope. We want her to come home but there is no closure. I've lived through death...in a bizarre kind of way, this is worse."

Laura Marie Nimbach was just 22 years old when she went missing from St. Petersburg, Florida in February 2009. A smart and friendly young woman, Laura had experienced some tough times but was on the road to recovery when she suddenly vanished. Laura has brown eyes and brown hair that she usually dyed blonde. At the time of her disappearance, Laura was 5 feet 5 inches tall and weighed 105 pounds. Her ears, nose, tongue, and upper lip are pierced and she has a pink flower tattoo on her lower back and "LN" tattooed on her left wrist. If you have any information about Laura, please contact the Pinellas County Sheriff's Office at 727-582-6333.

Patsy Nonemaker

When Patsy Nonemaker left her Shepherdsville, Kentucky, house around 4:00 pm on Friday, December 31, 1999, she wasn't in the best state of mind. The 55-year-old had struggled with depression and mental illness for years, and 1999 had been particularly rough for her. Her beloved dog went missing in September, and her father died on December 19th. Shortly after her father's death, her doctor increased the amount of medication she was taking; she was still adjusting to this dose when she walked out of her front door on New Year's Eve and vanished.

Patsy had spent much of Friday afternoon with her husband of 36 years, Paul Nonemaker. A few hours after the couple ate lunch, Paul left the house to run some errands. When he got home at 6:00 pm, he was surprised to discover that his wife wasn't at home. Her car was in the driveway and her purse was in the master bedroom, but Patsy was missing.

Due to Patsy's fragile mental condition, Paul was immediately concerned. Assuming that she had to be on foot, he drove slowly around the neighborhood, searching in vain for any sign of Patsy. A couple of Paul's neighbors recalled seeing Patsy; she had asked them if they had seen her missing dog. When they told her that they hadn't, she walked off. They last saw her heading down Lees Valley Way toward Highway 44 shortly after 4:00 pm.

Patsy's dog had been missing for several months and the neighborhood had been searched several times, but it was possible that, in her fragile mental state, Patsy had decided to make another attempt at locating her beloved pet. Paul noted that Patsy had taken the dog's disappearance hard. "She was already very depressed, and that dog was her companion while I was at work."

As darkness fell and the temperature dropped, Paul grew increasingly worried about Patsy's safety. She had wandered away from home before – one time she managed to make her way to Michigan – but she had always taken her purse and other belongings with her. This time, she left the house with nothing but the clothes on her back. Her wallet, keys, identification, and all other personal items were left behind.

Paul called the Bullitt County Sheriff's Department and reported his wife missing. Despite the fact that Patsy suffered from mental illness, the sheriff's department told Paul that she was an adult, free to come and go as she pleased. Detective Charles Mann told him that he would enter Patsy as an endangered missing person in a national database, but there was little he could do to locate her. Detective Mann admitted to a reporter, "I feel sorry for Paul, I don't know what to tell him."

Paul, who worked as a flight training supervisor for United Parcel Service, turned to some of his friends and co-workers for help locating his missing wife. Members of the International Pilots Association in Louisville offered to help distribute Patsy's missing posters throughout the county; they also placed a picture of Patsy and information about her case on their website.

The International Pilots Association helped Paul organize an extensive ground search for Patsy. Volunteers combed through the neighborhood, slowly walking each of the routes that Patsy might have used to get to the nearest highway. They found nothing.

As days went by without any word from Patsy, her

family feared the worst. Paul told reporters that Patsy had disappeared a few times in the past, but he was certain that this disappearance wasn't like the others. "I'm afraid someone has picked her up. Usually, when she disappears, she'll call me and tell me she's okay within four or five days." Weeks turned into months, and Patsy remained missing.

As news about Patsy's disappearance spread, investigators received a few tips concerning possible sightings of the missing woman. One came from a gas station attendant who worked on Highway 44; he told detectives that he was certain Patsy had stopped by the gas station the night she vanished. She had been asking people if they had seen her dog. The woman didn't appear to be in any sort of distress and the attendant didn't notice what direction she went when she left the gas station.

Paul did everything he could to gain publicity for his wife's disappearance, but he soon found that a missing adult wasn't considered newsworthy. He pleaded with several television shows – including America's Most Wanted, Dateline, and 20/20 – to run a feature about Patsy, but they all refused.

Desperate to find Patsy, Paul called the FBI for help. It was possible that Patsy had gotten into a vehicle that had taken her outside of Kentucky, but with no solid evidence to back up this theory, agents with the FBI told Paul that they had no jurisdiction over the case and couldn't offer any assistance.

For Paul, it was a frustrating experience; he just wanted to find his wife. "Most states will actively pursue missing children, but not adults. So it's like a dead end every time I try to pursue it. It's disheartening. I'm heartbroken about losing her. I know she walked away on her own, but she was not well."

Thanks to the help of the International Pilots Association, Patsy's missing person flyers were distributed across the country, and potential sightings of her were reported in several different states. Paul, desperate to find his wife, followed up on every report. He spent hours on the road, traveling as far as necessary to check out each possible sighting. None of them could be confirmed.

As the one-year anniversary of Patsy's disappearance approached, her family faced their first holiday season without her. On December 30, 1999, they decided to hold a celebration of life to honor Patsy. As hard as it was for them to admit it, none of Patsy's loved ones believed there was any chance she would be found alive.

Paul was sure that Patsy would have reached out to him if she were able to. "She's never not called us when she disappeared. She's not the type of person to hide from us if she was in her right mind. She is compassionate and concerned about us worrying for her."

Patsy's son, Timothy Nonemaker, didn't believe his mom was missing voluntarily. "Whenever she would leave, she would always call in a few days to let people know she was okay. But she didn't take her car or purse...she just walked off and disappeared."

Detective Mann told the family that investigators had exhausted all leads in Patsy's disappearance, and with no solid evidence suggesting foul play, there was nothing else that could be done. "We've done everything we can do."

Patsy's family was critical of law enforcement and their response to the disappearance. Timothy noted, "The police didn't do any investigation. If they had done something in the first 24 hours, when she was around here, they probably would have found her."

A year after Patsy was last seen, the Kentucky State Police Missing Persons Unit offered their assistance in the investigation. They made flyers with information about the case and sent them to each sheriff's office and police department in Kentucky and the seven bordering states. They also mailed Patsy's missing poster to Wal-Marts throughout the eight-state area as well as homeless shelters.

Patsy's loved ones appreciated the fact that the Kentucky State Police were willing to finally help, but worried that it was too late. Paul stated, "The trail is pretty cold now. We don't have much hope…" He vowed to keep searching on his own and continued to follow up on each potential sighting that was reported to him. Eventually, tips stopped coming in and Patsy's case went cold.

For Patsy's loved ones, the complete lack of information was devastating. In 2001, Paul admitted to a reporter, "Not knowing what happened to her, it's hard to have closure. This has been the roughest year of my life. I still miss her very much and am heartbroken about losing her. It's almost inexplicable that we still don't have any information on what happened."

Patsy has now been missing for more than two decades. There are several theories about what might have happened to her but no solid evidence to support any of them. It's possible that Patsy wandered off the highway while looking for her dog and got lost in a wooded area. She might have gotten a ride with someone who took advantage of her vulnerable state and killed her; she could have hitched a ride to the nearest city and blended in with the homeless population. Cold case detectives continue to hope that someone will come forward with the information they need to finally determine what happened to Patsy.

Patsy Ruth Nonemaker was 55 years old when she walked away from her home in Shepherdsville, Kentucky on New Year's Eve 1999. Patsy suffered from depression and other mental illnesses, and she had wandered away from home several times before, but she always contacted her family within a few days and made arrangements to be picked up. Patsy has brown eyes and brown hair, and at the time of her disappearance, she was 5 feet 2 inches tall and weighed 140 pounds. Patsy was last seen wearing gray pants, a blue or gray shirt, a white scarf, and brown suede shoes; her long, black overcoat was missing from the home and it is believed she was wearing it. She was also wearing several pieces of jewelry, including a diamond and gold wedding ring and a heart-shaped diamond necklace. Patsy has a mole on her left cheek and her right index finger is shorter than normal. If you have any information about Patsy, please contact the Bullitt County Sheriff's Department at 502-543-2514.

Lance Perkins

Lance Perkins, a 43-year-old art director from Anaheim, California, didn't feel well on the evening of Sunday, October 23, 2016. He had been in San Diego, California, for a few days to work at the Casa de las Calaveras event when he started feeling ill and went back to his room at the Cosmopolitan Hotel. Lance called his mother, Donna Perkins, around 7:00 pm on Sunday and told her that he had been experiencing blackouts. Donna was immediately concerned. "I told him he had to go to the hospital right away."

After speaking with his mom, Lance called 911 and an ambulance was dispatched to his hotel. After explaining his symptoms to paramedics, Lance was transported to the University of California at San Diego Medical Center's emergency room for evaluation.

Exactly what happened after Lance arrived at the hospital is shrouded in mystery and it's unclear if he received any treatment while he was there. At 10:00 pm, seemingly frustrated by the long wait time to see a doctor, Lance walked out of the hospital. Since he had been brought to the hospital by ambulance, he was without a vehicle and had no transportation back to his hotel. Rather than try to call around to get a ride, Lance simply left the hospital on foot.

The hospital, located in the Hillcrest neighborhood of San Diego, was about four miles away from the Cosmopolitan Hotel where Lance was staying. It's unknown where Lance was headed when he left the emergency room – he may have planned on walking back to his hotel – but surveillance cameras outside the hospital captured the initial steps of his journey.

When Lance walked out of the emergency room, camera footage shows that he headed north on Front Street, then turned left on Dickinson Street. This took him behind the hospital and away from the main highway running through the area. He was last seen on surveillance footage at 10:21 pm, walking along Dickinson Street as it curved towards the west.

Lance never made it back to his hotel that night. Donna realized something was wrong when she was unable to get in touch with her son on Monday. She and Lance's father, Jerry Perkins, lived in Hawaii but were always in daily contact with their son. After repeated attempts to call his cell phone, the hospital, and his hotel room, Donna started reaching out to some of Lance's friends. No one was able to shed any light on his whereabouts, so Donna called the San Diego Police Department and reported Lance missing.

San Diego detectives visited the hospital where Lance was last seen, but due to HIPAA regulations they came away with only limited information about what had happened in the emergency room Sunday night. It's still unclear if Lance left the hospital because of the long wait or if he was released after being seen by a doctor, but the general consensus is that he left before a provider was able to evaluate him.

Lance's cell phone records showed that he made numerous calls after leaving the hospital; ominously, seven of these calls were made to 911. Officials have never released the content of these 911 calls, but two of them were rather lengthy: there was one call that lasted 14 minutes and a second one that was 17 minutes long.

Around 4:00 am Monday, there were phone calls made from Lance's phone to two of his friends, but neither one heard their phone ring and the calls went to voicemail. Lance didn't leave a message for either friend; according to Donna, all that could be heard was a whooshing sound, as if Lance were moving at the time of the call. It's possible that he had his phone in his pocket and didn't realize he had dialed anyone. The last call from his phone was at 6:16 am; after that, he either turned the phone off or the battery died.

Lance's loved ones immediately organized a search for the missing man. They created a Facebook page to raise awareness about the case and printed missing person flyers that they distributed throughout the San Diego area. Donna was especially concerned because Lance had several medical conditions – including asthma – that required daily medication. "He's had a number of ailments and issues since he was young." Going without his prescriptions for any length of time would put his health at risk.

A search of the area surrounding the hospital yielded no sign of Lance. Search dogs were used to comb through nearby Bachman Canyon, which was located just north of where Lance was last seen on Dickinson Street; they found nothing to indicate Lance had been there. Police in Anaheim searched Lance's apartment to see if they could find any clues to his whereabouts but came up empty. Lance had seemingly vanished without a trace.

Weeks passed without any progress on the case. As the holidays approached, Lance's loved ones continued to do everything they could to make sure the public knew he was still missing, but the case attracted little media attention. Although there were a few potential sightings of the missing man, none of them could be confirmed and

Donna didn't believe her son was wandering the streets. "If he were on the street, he'd be dead. He hasn't refilled his prescriptions in two months or used his debit cards."

After checking with morgues and jails in both California and Mexico without finding anyone matching Lance's description, investigators concluded that the missing man was most likely in a hospital somewhere. For detectives, it was the theory that made the most sense; they had been unable to find any evidence pointing to foul play and Lance's fragile health made it likely that he had sought out medical treatment.

Months went by and there was still no word from Lance. His family was certain that he would have reached out to them if at all possible; the fact that he hadn't made some wonder if he was suffering from memory loss and didn't know his own name.

Donna was adamant that her son wouldn't have voluntarily disappeared, pointing out that he called 911 seven times right before he vanished. "Somebody who was planning on disappearing would not call 911 that many times." In a March 2017 interview with Dateline, she admitted that the passage of time wasn't making the situation any easier. "It's been difficult. Very difficult...people don't just go 'poof' and disappear." Lance, however, seems to have done just that.

Lance Perkins was 43 years old when he went missing in San Diego in 2016. The investigation into his disappearance went cold almost immediately and no new information about the case has been released in years. Lance has green eyes and brown hair, and at the time of his disappearance, he was 6 feet 1 inch tall and weighed 180 pounds. He was last seen wearing a black jacket, tan pants, and tan shoes; he sometimes wears eyeglasses. The circumstances surrounding his disappearance are clouded in mystery; it's possible he is suffering from memory loss and doesn't know his name. If you have any information about Lance, please contact the San Diego Police Department at 619-531-2844.

Pepita Redhair

Pepita Redhair had lunch with her mother, Anita King, on the afternoon of Tuesday, March 24, 2020. Anita then dropped Pepita off at her boyfriend's home in Albuquerque, New Mexico, a two-hour drive from Pepita's family home in Crownpoint, New Mexico. As Pepita got out of the car, she turned back to Anita and said, "Mom, I love you. Take care of yourself. Drive home safely." The 27-year-old gave her mom a final wave and went inside. Anita had no idea it would be the last time she would see her daughter.

Pepita had been living with her boyfriend, Nicholas Kaye, and his parents for more than three years, but she remained in constant contact with her family and visited them often. Anita noted, "She always called me every day, saying, 'Mom, what are you doing? What are you up to? Do you need anything?" Pepita would frequently end her day by sending Anita a goodnight text message. It was unheard of for her to be out of contact for an extended amount of time.

When Anita didn't hear from her daughter that Wednesday, her motherly intuition told her that something was wrong. She sent Pepita a text message asking if everything was okay but didn't get a response. As hours went by without any word from Pepita, Anita grew increasingly concerned. By Thursday, she was frantic.

Anita finally got a hold of Nick on Friday, and she asked him where her daughter was. Nick claimed that he had no idea; he insisted that he and Pepita had gotten into a fight while at a house party on Thursday night and she had left with another man. Anita was skeptical of his story, as she was certain that Pepita would have called her to let her know if she was staying anywhere other than Nick's house.

That same day, Anita received a text message from Pepita's phone, but it wasn't from her daughter. Instead, it was from a man who said he didn't know Pepita and had recently purchased the phone from someone else. To Anita, this meant that Pepita's phone had either been stolen from her or taken from her by someone who harmed her.

Fearful that Nick was responsible for Pepita's disappearance, Anita called the Albuquerque Police Department and attempted to report her daughter missing. Incredibly, police refused to do anything. "The cops just kind of brushed it off. They said she's an adult...she's free to travel, free to go missing...I was pretty upset." Anita insisted that Pepita was not the type of person to voluntarily stay out of contact with her family; she was certain that something terrible had happened to her. Once again, police brushed her off and assured her that Pepita would come back when she was ready. They told her to give it a week or two and call back if she was still missing.

Anita and Pepita's sister, Shelda Livingston, were angered and dismayed by the lack of concern on the part of the Albuquerque Police Department, especially since they were aware of the fact that there was a history of domestic violence between Nick and Pepita. Officers had been to Nick's home after a particularly violent confrontation just six weeks before Pepita vanished; Nick had assaulted Pepita so badly that she was hospitalized. Anita and Shelda were convinced that Nick was directly responsible for Pepita's disappearance and couldn't understand why police seemed uninterested in interviewing him about his missing girlfriend.

Terrified that Nick might be holding her younger sister against her will, Shelda drove to the quiet cul-de-sac where he lived and approached the concrete barrier that served as a fence. She yelled for her sister, begging her to come outside. The only response she got was from Nick's dogs, who barked loudly at the intrusion. At one point Shelda saw one of the curtains inside move as if someone were peering out the window, but no one came out to talk to her. Defeated, she returned home.

Hoping that the Navajo Nation police force in Crownpoint would be more helpful, Anita called them and tried to get them to take a missing person report. They told her that since Pepita had last been seen in Albuquerque, they had no jurisdiction in the case. They referred Anita back to the Albuquerque Police Department.

Anita once again called the Albuquerque police, but they remained unhelpful and she could tell that they didn't care about Pepita. "They said my daughter was a drunk. They assumed that she was gone [voluntarily] and that she was not important." She noted that their lackadaisical response was likely a result of systemic racism that existed in the police department. "Us Native Americans are pushed away and our voices are not taken seriously. We are not acknowledged."

Shelda contacted local news stations, asking them to air a picture of Pepita so the public would know that she was missing. None of the stations were willing to help. "That's when we realized...we have to do this on our own."

Frustrated, Anita and Shelda decided to launch their own search for Pepita. They had limited resources, but with the help of other family members, they were able to scrape up enough money to make missing person flyers emblazoned with pictures of Pepita. They then traveled to Albuquerque and hung them up throughout the area where Pepita had last been seen. Pepita didn't have her own car and usually relied on public transportation to get places, so they made sure to hang up posters at bus stations, hoping that somehow Pepita might see one and know that they were looking for her.

Anita and Shelda knocked on doors in Nick's neighborhood, handing out missing posters and asking residents if anyone had seen Pepita recently. Most of the locals knew Pepita – who they described as being a nice, friendly, young woman – but none of them had seen her since she had been reported missing.

Two weeks after Pepita was last seen, her family organized a physical search of Albuquerque's West Mesa neighborhood. Although part of the area had been developed into subdivisions, searchers concentrated on the vast desert area on the outskirts of the city. Anita and Shelda feared that Nick had killed Pepita and then dumped her body somewhere in the desert. It was like looking for a needle in a haystack.

Hoping to make their search a little easier, the family asked Albuquerque police if it would be possible for them to use cadaver dogs to hunt for Pepita's remains. Their request was denied. Instead, family members used sticks to open up any garbage bags they found in the desert, unsure if they really wanted to see what was inside. They found nothing that led them any closer to Pepita.

On April 19th, nearly a month after Pepita was last seen, Nick went to the Albuquerque Police Department and reported his girlfriend missing. It's unclear why he waited so long to do so; Nick has never granted any requests for interviews. In his report, he stated that he last saw Pepita on March 26th; they had an argument at a party in Albuquerque and she left on foot with a male named Laramy.

According to Nick, he got a text message from Pepita's phone the following day; the message stated that Pepita was with another man and was not coming back. Nick told police he assumed that the man the text message referred to was Laramy; he also stated that the grammar and tone of the text message made him believe that it was written by Pepita.

Oddly, police appear to have taken Nick's statement at face value; he was never re-interviewed, but investigators declared that he was not a suspect in Pepita's disappearance. Even odder, they made no attempt to locate Laramy and question him to see if he had indeed been the last person seen with Pepita.

Anita was blunt about her feelings towards the Albuquerque Police Department. "They didn't do a proper investigation. They didn't do an interview with the entire family or the boyfriend." She wasn't willing to let her daughter's case slip through the cracks. "Even though I might have to foot search on my own, I'm still going to do it. I need to have my daughter home."

Hoping to drum up some leads and locate the mysterious Laramy, Pepita's family members made several posts on Facebook. Their strategy worked, and they were soon contacted by Laramy. He told them that he did indeed know Pepita, but had last seen her on March 10th, two weeks before she went missing. He was certain of the date because it had been his birthday and Pepita had bought him a cupcake to celebrate. He noted that she had been with Nick at the time, and he seemed to get upset when she presented Laramy with the cupcake and sang "Happy Birthday" to him. According to Laramy, Nick was so angry over the incident that he hit Pepita. Uncomfortable with what was going on, Laramy claimed he left the couple at that point. He never heard from Pepita again.

If what Laramy said was true, Nick had lied in his police report when he claimed that Pepita left the party with Laramy on March 26th. If Nick was telling the truth, it would mean that Laramy was lying when he told Anita he hadn't seen Pepita after March 10th. Unfortunately, investigators never followed up with either man, and Laramy died not long after he contacted Anita. It was almost as if the Albuquerque Police Department didn't want the case to be solved.

Despite the lack of response from Albuquerque investigators, Anita continued to call them nearly every day. Citing the growing COVID-19 crisis, detectives claimed that they were unable to conduct interviews with any potential witnesses. While there were numerous COVID-related restrictions in place at the time, investigators never even bothered to conduct any phone interviews with Nick, his parents, or any members of Pepita's family. Anita and Shelda were forced to conduct their own investigation without any help from law enforcement.

Anita and Shelda continued to hang up missing person flyers and solicit leads on Facebook. On May 20th, Shelda was contacted by a woman who claimed that Pepita was seen in Albuquerque's City Park. The woman hung up before Shelda could get any additional information from her. Shelda immediately drove to Albuquerque and scoured City Park for any sign of her sister, even showing her picture to any person she came across, but found nothing to suggest that Pepita had been there.

When she left the park, she noticed that there were several men with walkie-talkies seemingly keeping watch over the parking lot of a nearby hotel. Shelda drove into the parking lot and noticed a line of vans with darkly tinted windows; it appeared the men were keeping a close eye on these vans. Shelda sensed something was off about the situation and wondered if the vans were being used in human trafficking. It was a sickening possibility.

Near the end of May, Anita was able to retrieve Pepita's belongings from Nick's house. Most of the items were placed in Pepita's old bedroom in her mother's Crownpoint home, but Shelda put some of her clothing in a plastic bag and took it to a Navajo medicine man, who conducted a Navajo ceremony in an attempt to see what had happened to Pepita. The man told Shelda that her little sister was still alive, but was being held somewhere against her will and unable to return home. It was a heartbreaking thought, but it gave Pepita's family some hope that she would one day be reunited with them.

On June 10th, Shelda received a call from a woman who thought they had seen Pepita outside of a supermarket. As she had with the last tip, Shelda immediately dropped everything she was doing and raced to the location of the reported sighting. She saw a woman who looked so much like Pepita that she chased after her, yelling for her to stop. When she got closer, her heart sank. Although the woman looked exactly like Pepita, she was taller and didn't have any tattoos. Shelda apologized and told the woman that she looked like her missing sister, and the woman said she had been stopped several times by people who thought she was Pepita. It seemed likely that Pepita had never been in this area; the tipster had likely seen her lookalike.

Months went by with little progress in the

investigation. Anita and Shelda did everything they could to make sure that people were aware that Pepita was still missing, but they continued to be frustrated by the apathy of the Albuquerque Police Department. By March 2021, Pepita had been missing for a year and law enforcement still hadn't conducted even a cursory investigation into her disappearance.

Anita's frustration with the investigation reached a head in early September 2021, when the case of Gabby Petito made headlines across the nation. Gabby – a 22-year-old white woman from Florida – went missing while on a cross-country trip with her boyfriend and was last seen in Wyoming. When her parents, who lived in New York, reported her missing after not hearing from her for several days, law enforcement immediately launched an extensive investigation into her disappearance. While Anita had nothing but sympathy for Gabby's family – she knew what it felt like to be missing a daughter – she was angered by the fact that Pepita's case hadn't even been deemed worthy of making the local news, let alone receive national coverage. It was inherently unfair.

Anita was briefly distracted from her hunt for Pepita when, on September 28, 2021, her husband – Pepita's father – died. "He didn't get closure...that was kind of the saddest thing. I promised him that we are going to find our daughter." Anita vowed to intensify her efforts to locate Pepita.

On October 3, 2021, the family organized a rally in Albuquerque's Tiguex Park. Although Anita had initially planned the rally as a way of bringing attention to Pepita's disappearance, the event soon took on a life of its own when the Missing and Murdered Indigenous Women organization got involved. The families of dozens of missing Native American women showed up to take part in the rally; each family told a similar story about how law enforcement had brushed them off when they tried to get help.

Bernalillo County District Attorney Raul Torrez spoke at the event, telling the crowd, "We owe it to one another to do everything we can to make sure that these women come home." In addition, he agreed to have his office take over Pepita's case.

The District Attorney's Office immediately set about doing the basic tasks that law enforcement should have done in the days following Pepita's disappearance. Warrants were filed for phone records and other electronic media, and a DNA profile for Pepita was entered into a national database so it could be compared against any unidentified dead bodies that had been found since she went missing.

D.A. Torrez was realistic about Pepita's case. "A year and a half is a very long gap for us in terms of the timeline that we usually like to engage in. We remain optimistic but at this point, I don't have any answers about what happened to her."

Anita was grateful for the help but noted that it was unclear if any progress had been made on the case as investigators wouldn't release any information. "They say it's confidential because the case is still active." It was frustrating for the family to be kept in the dark after spending 18 months investigating the case on their own, but they tried to remain hopeful that they would soon have answers.

In October 2022, authorities announced that they were offering a $2,000 reward for information leading to Pepita's whereabouts. Her family believes that someone out there has the information needed to bring Pepita home and hopes that the offer of a reward will bring in some new leads.

Anita has spoken at several events regarding missing Native American women and prays that law enforcement will start listening to the families of the missing. "I hope they hear our cry. We want to be taken seriously."

Pepita Redhair was 27 years old when she went missing from Albuquerque, New Mexico in March 2020. A happy young woman with an infectious laugh, she loved skateboarding, drawing, and cooking; she hoped to one day become an engineer or a teacher. She was taking classes at a local community college and worked part-time at Hot Topic in Albuquerque, and she remained in constant contact with her mother and sister. The circumstances surrounding her disappearance are unclear, but her family is certain she was a victim of foul play. Pepita has brown eyes and brown hair, and at the time of her disappearance, she was 5 feet 1 inch tall and weighed 140 pounds. She has a tattoo of a dinosaur on her right forearm, a koi fish on her left forearm, a moon on her left leg, and a butterfly on her shoulder. If you have any information about Pepita, please contact the Bernalillo County Sheriff's Office at 505-222-1101.

Alexis Scott

Alexis Scott put her 2-year-old son to bed around 8:00 pm on Friday, September 22, 2017, but she wasn't ready to call it an early night. The 20-year-old, who lived with her mother and brother in Peoria, Illinois, spent much of the evening messaging some of her friends on Facebook, then left the house to meet up with some of them shortly before midnight. She told her brother she would see him later, then headed out into the mild night air. She never made it back home.

April was surprised when she woke up Saturday morning and discovered that her daughter was gone. The two of them had plans to do some things together that weekend, so April sent Alexis a few text messages asking where she was and when she was coming home. Although she was somewhat concerned when she got no response, she tried to shrug it off. Alexis was a social young woman and it wasn't unheard of for her to spend the night with friends when she knew her mother was at home to watch her son. April assumed that she would hear from Alexis soon enough.

By Sunday, April was starting to grow increasingly worried. It was unusual for Alexis to fail to respond to text messages, and she hadn't posted anything on any of her social media accounts since very early on Saturday morning. Worried that something was seriously wrong, April reached out to some of her daughter's friends on Facebook but no one was able to tell her anything about her whereabouts.

April stopped at a gas station on Monday and ran into two men Alexis knew there. She asked them if they had spoken to Alexis recently; one man told her that he had gone out with her for a while on Friday night but parted ways with her early Saturday morning because she wanted to go to a party. He hadn't heard anything from her since then.

The other man initially claimed that he had dropped Alexis off at a home on West Richmond Avenue after first taking her home to change her clothes. When April checked with her son, however, he was adamant that Alexis hadn't stopped by the house to change. Since she had recently lost her house keys, she wouldn't have been able to get into the house unless her brother unlocked the door for her. He had been home all night but Alexis did not return.

Confused about the conflicting stories, April made several more attempts to reach Alexis, warning her that if she didn't hear back from her she was going to report her missing. She spent a sleepless night waiting for Alexis to contact her but never heard a word. Convinced that something terrible had happened to her daughter, April called the Peoria Police Department and filed a missing person report.

An officer was dispatched to April's home to speak with her, and she told him what she had learned from the men she saw at the gas station. The officer said he was going to speak with the men and would get back to her. According to April, when the officer contacted her later, he seemed shaken by what he had learned and told her that he was going to classify Alexis as an endangered missing person.

Detectives interviewed the people who had attended the party where Alexis was last seen. Partygoers told conflicting stories about when Alexis arrived and how long she stayed. Although one of her male friends had told April he dropped Alexis off at the home, police later interviewed a Lyft driver who said she had been the one who took Alexis to the party. At the time of her disappearance, Alexis did not have her own vehicle and would often book rides with this particular Lyft driver, who told police she knew Alexis fairly well. She recalled dropping Alexis off at the home on West Richmond Avenue around 4:30 am Saturday.

Some of the people who attended the party thought they saw Alexis leave on foot sometime after 5:30 am, though they gave conflicting stories about which direction she went when she left. One man claimed he saw Alexis get into a dark blue Chevrolet Impala; he later changed his story and said he had been in the backyard when she left, meaning he wouldn't have been able to see if Alexis had gotten into a car or not. A couple of females told investigators that they had been on the front porch and saw Alexis get into a dark-colored car with tinted windows.

Investigators were able to obtain surveillance footage from several cameras in the area surrounding the home where the party was held. Peoria Police Detective Matt Rogers told reporters that this footage did not back up the witness accounts. "We interviewed everyone that was involved with this party. A couple of people admitted to seeing Alexis leave shortly after she arrived...video footage that we had removed from local businesses did not match what they had told us."

Armed with these inconsistencies, detectives re-interviewed the partygoers. Several of them admitted that they had been intoxicated at the time and could have been mistaken about when and how Alexis left. Whether these witnesses were honestly confused or deliberately hiding something, they were of little use to investigators.

On October 1, 2017, detectives received the homeowner's consent to search the house where the party had been held but found no clues to Alexis's whereabouts. They also obtained her cell phone records and learned that her phone had last been used at 5:09 am on Saturday. Investigators attempted to ping the phone in order to determine its location but were unable to do so; the phone had either been turned off or had a dead battery.

April wasn't content to sit back and wait for police to find her daughter; she immediately launched a concurrent search of her own. She gathered friends and family members, printed missing person flyers, and canvassed the neighborhood where Alexis had last been seen, desperate for any information about Alexis. Anytime she learned of a potential tip, she called detectives so they could follow up on it.

The week after Alexis was last seen, April told reporters, "I just wanna know where my daughter is. I'm not pointing fingers, I know [there was] a party, I know kids do things at parties we may not necessarily approve of." She had only one goal: to find Alexis. "I want to know that she's okay. I need to know that she's safe."

April – and investigators – soon realized that Alexis's disappearance was possibly linked to a trip she had taken to Las Vegas the previous month, when what Alexis thought would be a fun weekend away turned into an absolute nightmare.

Alexis and a friend had agreed to go to Las Vegas with a party promoter they met through Facebook who was hiring dancers and models to act as "eye candy" at a bachelor's party. April had told her daughter that she didn't think it was a good idea, but Alexis was determined to go as she thought it would be an easy way to make some money. The man purchased plane tickets for the two girls and accompanied them to Las Vegas, where everything fell apart.

When the girls got there, they were told that the bachelor's party had been canceled. It's unclear exactly what happened next, but at some point Alexis was separated from her friend and missed her flight back to Illinois. Her friend and the man who hired them made the flight home but seemingly had no idea where Alexis had gone.

April had no idea that anything was wrong until she got a phone call from Sacramento, California; a woman there had found Alexis, naked and terrified, on a street and immediately recognized that she needed help. The frightened young woman told her that she had been kidnapped and forced into prostitution but had managed to escape, albeit without any of her belongings. The good Samaritan bought Alexis some clothing at a nearby Wal-Mart and helped her get in touch with her mother.

When Alexis finally spoke with April, she didn't give her many details about what had happened, only that she missed her flight and needed a way back to Chicago. April arranged for her to take a Greyhound bus back to Chicago and some friends picked her up at the bus station. April noticed that her daughter had bruises on her body when she arrived home, but Alexis didn't want to talk about how she got them.

After Alexis disappeared from the party, April started to learn more about what had actually happened to her in Las Vegas. Alexis had confided in friends that she believed she had been drugged, then she was abducted and taken to California; some of these friends finally opened up to April and told her that her daughter had been a victim of human trafficking and had been fearful that her abductor would somehow find her and force her back into prostitution.

April became convinced that the party promoter who arranged for Alexis to go to Las Vegas had been behind her abduction there; ominously, the owner of the home where Alexis was last seen was a friend of this man. April was certain that her daughter had once again become a victim of human trafficking and was determined to prove it.

Although detectives were open to the idea that Alexis had been trafficked, they lacked any evidence to back up this claim. Hoping to find potential witnesses, investigators went door-to-door in the neighborhood where the party was held but failed to find anyone who admitted to seeing Alexis. Fearing that she hadn't made it out of the house alive, they searched vacant homes in the area looking for any sign of her body. They found nothing.

In November, they returned to the home where the party was held. According to Peoria Police Captain Michael Mushinsky, "We weren't getting a lot of information so we ended up doing a search warrant at that address...we collected some stuff but nothing that stood out."

As the investigation stretched into its second month, April admitted, "I feel like I'm in a nightmare that cannot possibly be my life." She was doing everything she could to raise awareness about her daughter's disappearance but felt that police weren't doing their part to find Alexis. Captain Mushinsky disputed this, telling reporters, "We've definitely been pretty aggressive in how we're working it. We're following up on every lead we get."

Eventually, a man came forward and told investigators a disturbing story. He claimed that the owner of the West Richmond Avenue house had called him the morning after the party because he needed to get rid of some items from the home. The informant said he had been hired to drive a U-Haul from the house to an isolated area near Canton, Illinois, where the items, which included a mattress and some carpet, were burned.

Detective Matt Rogers admitted that it would be unusual for someone to travel that far outside the city to burn trash. "[It's] concerning, because it was the same morning that Alexis had gone missing." Although the informant hadn't seen a body, according to April, he claimed "he opened the U-Haul door and there was more blood than he had ever seen in his life." The implication was that Alexis had been killed in the home.

A search of the area described by the informant was soon underway, and investigators did find a burn pit containing items matching those supposedly removed from the home. The Illinois State Police conducted forensic testing on the items, and cadaver dogs were used to search the burn pit and the surrounding area. They found no clues to Alexis's whereabouts.

Alexis's loved ones were forced to endure the holiday season without her. By February, April was fed up with the lack of progress on the case and intensified her own efforts to find out what had happened to her daughter. She held a fundraiser, hoping to bring in enough money to hire a private investigator, and did everything she could to keep the case in the news.

Months went by without any breaks in the case. On the first anniversary of the disappearance, family and friends held a march to make sure people knew that Alexis was still missing. They marched straight to the home where Alexis had seemingly vanished from, where a short scuffle broke out between marchers and residents of the home. The marchers were demanding to know where Alexis was, while the residents continued to deny they had any information about the case.

By the second anniversary, hope was starting to fade. Although April still wanted to believe that Alexis was alive, she admitted that it seemed unlikely. "I have to be truthful...the information that we have turned over and the information that police have, it's always been that she's deceased." Still, she continued organizing searches, desperate to bring her daughter home.

Alexis has been missing for more than five years now, and detectives don't know much more than they did on the day she was reported missing. They have served more than 20 search warrants and followed up on hundreds of leads but none have brought them any closer to finding Alexis. Some investigators believe that Alexis was a victim of human trafficking, others believe she was killed at the home where the party was held. April just wants closure. "I don't want death to be the closure, but if that's where we are, I want those responsible to be held accountable."

Alexis Camry Scott was just 20 years old when she went missing from Peoria, Illinois in September 2017. A vibrant and social young woman, she was close with her mother and siblings and adored her 2-year-old son. Her loved ones know she never would have willingly abandoned her family; they believe she could have been a victim of human trafficking. Alexis has brown eyes and black hair, and at the time of her disappearance, she was 5 feet 1 inch tall and weighed 115 pounds. She was last seen wearing blue jeans, a cropped top, and a black and pink hooded sweatshirt. Alexis has several tattoos, including the name "Tevin Jr" on her right collarbone, the name "Trevon" on her right wrist, the name "Lilly" on the left side of her collarbone, and the word "Royalty" on her left arm. If you have any information about Alexis, please contact the Peoria Police Department at 309-673-4521.

Eric Smith

Eric Smith left his Cedar Bluff, Virginia, home around 10:00 am Friday, November 8, 2013. The 41-year-old planned to spend the morning hunting on his rural property and told his wife that he would see her later that day. He had a deer stand located approximately a mile from their home, and his wife assumed that he was heading there. Shortly after Eric left, his wife and one of their two daughters traveled to his mother-in-law's home in Buchanan County and spent the day there. When they returned to Cedar Bluff early that evening, Eric wasn't at the house.

Eric hadn't been feeling well in the days leading up to his hunting excursion – he had been exhibiting flulike symptoms – so his wife was concerned when he wasn't home by sunset. Since he hadn't planned on being gone for long, Eric hadn't taken his cell phone with him when he left the house that morning, leaving his wife no way to get in contact with him.

As darkness fell, Eric's wife grew more concerned. She knew that Eric's mother, Dreama Smith, was attending Friday night church services nearby, so she drove there to see if anyone in Eric's family had heard from him that day. As soon as she saw her daughter-in-law, Dreama knew that something was wrong. She and other family members immediately left church. "We went directly to [Eric's] house...people from church followed us. They came up and people were in the woods looking for him."

Although temperatures had been mild that

afternoon, topping out in the fifties, as darkness settled over the area the temperature dropped dramatically and Eric's wife decided to call the police and report her husband missing.

Authorities immediately launched a search for Eric. Police officers, firefighters, and local volunteers scoured the area surrounding his property on Friday night but failed to find any trace of the missing man. Cedar Bluffs Police Chief David Mills admitted that the ground search was complicated by the fact that Eric had been wearing camouflage hunting apparel. "He could be lying down and he would be impossible to see." Worried that he could be concealed in the dense underbrush, a Virginia State Police helicopter equipped with FLIR thermal vision made several passes over the 40-acre area of land that constituted Eric's property. Unfortunately, the air search failed to find anything.

The hunt for Eric intensified on Saturday, with members of the Virginia State Police and the Consolidation Coal Company's mine rescue team joining the search party. Eric was a long-time employee of Consolidation and had been a member of the same mine rescue team that assisted in the search. They were determined to find their missing friend and coworker. David Queensberry, a member of the team, stated that they were trained in search and rescue and would search for any missing person, but admitted that the search for Eric was more personal. "Eric is one of us. He is one of our family."

Cedar Bluff councilman and firefighter James Brown had nothing but praise for the mine rescue team, noting that they stayed in a shoulder-to-shoulder formation as they searched to make sure they didn't miss anything in the rough terrain. "They're fearless. If they can't see the top of the person's foot beside them, that means they're too far apart." Long after many of the volunteer searchers had to return to their jobs and families, the mine rescue team continued their exhaustive search for Eric. They were heartbroken when they were unable to find any clues as to what might have happened to him.

Six tracking dogs were brought in to assist the searchers, and though they were able to pick up several scent trails leading away from Eric's home – and at least one returning to it – it was unclear which trail was the most recent. None of the trails led to Eric.

When Eric left the house that morning, he had been carrying only the 50-caliber muzzleloader he used for deer hunting. Officials assumed that the experienced hunter likely had one shot already loaded, so explosives detection dogs were brought in to see if they could hone in on the scent of gunpowder. The dogs spent hours combing through the woods but failed to find any trace of Eric or his muzzleloader.

The search continued for nearly a week and covered more than 800 acres, expanding throughout the area surrounding Cedar Bluff, Richlands, Claypool Hill, and Kent Ridge Road. Despite the massive effort, searchers found no clues leading to Eric's whereabouts. On Thursday, November 14, authorities announced that they were suspending the search for the missing hunter, though they would continue to investigate any new leads they received.

Detectives with the Cedar Bluff Police Department interviewed Eric's family members, friends, and co-workers, hoping to find some clue as to what might have happened to him. Cedar Bluff Police Chief David Mills noted that Eric wasn't the type of person one would expect to voluntarily go missing; he was described as being a hardworking man who was devoted to his family.

At the time of his disappearance, Eric was the general foreman at the Buchanan One coal mine. It was a position that carried a lot of responsibility; Eric was usually the first employee to arrive in the morning and the last one to leave in the evening. Mining is an inherently dangerous profession and Eric was responsible for making sure all state and federal safety regulations were promptly implemented and meticulously followed. According to coworkers, Eric was well-suited for the job and had earned the respect of his fellow employees.

At just 41 years old, Eric was young to be in a foreman position but fully qualified for the job. According to coworker Robert Baugh, Eric "went up the ladder fast. He was as good a mine operator as I ever had." It was a sentiment that was shared by many others who worked with the missing man. Virginia State Police Special Agent Jeff Stares told reporters that "not one person we talked to at the mines had an ill word to say about [Eric]. Everyone we talked to loved him to death."

Eric had earned a reputation for being a fair supervisor, one who treated everyone he interacted with equally. He was always willing to sit down and talk with his employees about any concerns or issues they might have. His position required him to be on call 24 hours a day in case any major issues arose at the mine, and he was used to taking calls from people at all hours of the day. He took the responsibility in stride and never complained.

As detectives went through the process of interviewing everyone who knew Eric and his family, it became clear that he had no reason to want to leave voluntarily. Investigators found no evidence of any problems at home or at work. Eric was completely dedicated to his wife and two children.

Although authorities initially seemed to lean towards the theory that Eric might have been injured in some kind of accident while out hunting, as days went by without any sign of his body or gun, they had to consider that his disappearance was possibly the result of foul play. Rumors about what might have happened to him made the rounds throughout his small town, with most of the locals agreeing that foul play seemed likely. They were certain that Eric never would have voluntarily left his family and job, and they didn't believe that he had gotten lost or injured in the woods.

Cedar Bluff Police Chief David Mills cautioned people about spreading rumors about the case and told reporters that investigators had been unable to rule out any possible scenario, including that Eric had voluntarily left. Until some shred of evidence could be found, detectives were keeping all options on the table, however unlikely they seemed to those who knew Eric best. Detectives admitted that they were aware of all the rumors surrounding the potential for foul play but refused to comment on them.

It seemed like everyone in the area was closely following Eric's case. Although Chief David Mills made it a point to give frequent updates about the status of the search, it wasn't enough for some people. In the first 10 days of the investigation, so many people called 911 to ask for information about the case that the Tazewell County Sheriff's Office had to issue a statement pleading with the public to only utilize the emergency number for actual emergencies.

Although Eric's family continued to pray for his safe return, they knew he would never willingly miss celebrating Thanksgiving with his family and there was a noticeable pall when the holiday came and went without any progress on the case. December 3rd – Eric's 42nd birthday – also passed without any word about the missing man.

A month after Eric was last seen, his family announced that they were offering a $5,000 reward for any information leading to his location or recovery. Although a few tips trickled in to investigators, none of them led to Eric. Three weeks later, the Smith family increased the reward to $8,000.

As 2013 came to a close, the Smith family was left in limbo, wondering what had happened to Eric. Chief Mills told reporters that "Christmas was a sad and difficult time for the Smith family as they continue to worry about their loved one. His absence during the holidays only heightens the family's concern about Eric's safety and whereabouts."

Eric's employer soon announced that they were going to match the $8,000 being offered by Eric's family, bringing the total reward to $16,000. Cathy St. Clair, the Public Affairs Director for the company, stated, "We hope that the increase in the reward will help law enforcement in its efforts to solve this case." Members of the public also offered donations, and by the end of the month, the reward was up to nearly $18,000.

In April 2014, a tip line established by the Virginia State Police received a call from a person who claimed that Eric's body would be found near Daw Road, located close to the border between Tazewell and Russell counties. Investigators searched the area but failed to find anything related to Eric's disappearance.

By September 2014, Eric had been missing for ten months, and his family continued to do everything possible to keep his case in the public eye. Dreama told reporters that Eric's wife and children were having a hard time dealing with the disappearance, but they were all relying on their faith to carry them through. "We pray every day that something will open up." Although Dreama tried to remain optimistic, it was evident she was in pain. "There is a constant ache, constant sickness in your heart and stomach 24/7. It's unimaginable. Nobody should have to go through this. Nobody."

Investigators continued to actively work on Eric's case, but Chief Mills admitted that they had little to go on. "Every day somebody is working this, either my department or the Virginia State Police. We also have an FBI agent or two assisting us. We haven't forgotten Eric or his family."

As the first anniversary of Eric's disappearance approached, investigators received a call from a woman who believed she had seen the missing man in Buchanan County. Detectives immediately followed up on the lead but found nothing to suggest that Eric was in that area.

Eric's friends and family held a prayer vigil on November 8, 2014, to mark the grim anniversary of the last time they had seen him. Family friend Patsy Clifton noted that the vigil was a way "to remind people that we are still trying to come up with some answers. The family needs closure. More than 200 people attended to show their support for Eric's loved ones.

For Eric's family, it had been a heartbreaking year and the uncertainty was devastating. "I've imagined everything...that he got hurt, that somebody shot him during hunting season...but if that had been the case I think they would have found him." Dreama vowed that she would never stop looking for her oldest son. "It hasn't gotten any easier. People say time heals all wounds...I just don't see a way."

Chief Mills joined the family in remembering Eric.

"Even 12 months later not a day goes by that I don't think of Eric." He appealed to the public for help, noting that despite running down every lead they received, detectives still lacked the information needed to solve the case. "We truly need the public's help to bring him home."

Unfortunately, no new information came in and Eric's case gradually faded from the headlines. His family continued to pray daily for his return and hold vigils each November on the anniversary of his disappearance, but it was clear his case had stalled. Detectives admitted that they had no idea what had happened to the missing man.

In April 2016, investigators conducted a search of a mine located in the Red Ash area of Tazewell County after receiving a tip that Eric's body would be found there. Cadaver dogs were brought in to comb through the mine, which hadn't been active for more than three decades. Despite an intensive search, nothing was found.

Dreama remained in constant contact with law enforcement over the years. Although they had been unable to determine what had happened to her son, she had nothing but praise for the detectives working on the case. "They have checked everything. They have questioned everybody. They found nothing."

In November 2022, nine years after Eric was last seen, investigators announced that the case was no longer being considered a disappearance; detectives believed Eric had been murdered and Virginia State Police Special Agent Russell Edwards told reporters the case was being investigated as a homicide. No further details have been released, and Eric's loved ones continue to pray that they will one day get closure.

Eric Grady Smith was 41 years old when he went missing from Cedar Bluff, Virginia, in 2013. An avid hunter, he left his home to do some hunting on his property and never returned; his cell phone, cigarettes, wallet, and other personal belongings were left behind. Eric has brown hair and brown eyes, and at the time of his disappearance, he was 6 feet 1 inch tall and weighed 210 pounds. He was last seen wearing camouflage hunting clothing and a Timex watch; he was carrying a 50-caliber muzzleloader. If you have any information about Eric, please contact the Tazewell County Sheriff's Office at 276-988-0645.

Tonee Turner

Tonee Turner was her usual friendly self when she stopped by Dobra Tea in the Squirrel Hill section of Pittsburgh, Pennsylvania around 6:00 pm on Monday, December 30, 2019. The 22-year-old then got on a city bus headed for Pittsburgh's Hazelwood neighborhood where she lived. The bus driver noted that she got off at her normal stop on Giddings Street, but what happened to her after that is a mystery. She never made it home and was never seen again.

Monday night, a Pittsburgh firefighter riding his bike on the Homestead Grays Bridge found a purse on the pedestrian walkway of the bridge. Oddly, sitting next to the purse was a pair of shoes and a ceramic pot. Not seeing anyone on the bridge at the time, the cyclist took the purse home with him; he left the shoes and vase behind. He checked the contents of the purse for anything that might identify the owner and found a cell phone, keys, a water bottle, and a journal.

The following morning, the man called one of the phone numbers he found on the cell phone and reached Tonee's aunt. He explained that he had found the phone and other belongings on the bridge and was trying to reunite them with their owner. Tonee's aunt identified the phone as belonging to her niece, and the man returned all of the items to Tonee's family Tuesday morning.

The firefighter told Tonee's family that he had seen a pair of shoes and a ceramic vase next to the purse but had been unable to carry them back on his bicycle and assumed they were still on the bridge. Oddly, when family members went to retrieve these items, they were gone. It's unknown who removed them from the bridge; repeated public appeals for this person to come forward have gone unanswered. Since the items have never been recovered, no one can say for certain if they actually belonged to Tonee or not.

Tonee's family members were confused by the fact that Tonee's belongings had been found on the Homestead Grays Bridge, which was not in a part of town where she would normally be walking around. Tonee was known for losing her phone, however, so it was possible she had left her purse on the bus and someone else had picked it up.

Tonee's mother, Darlene Johnson, tried to reach Tonee at her Hazelwood home Tuesday morning but got no answer. She then started calling friends and other family members to see if any of them knew where Tonee was.

Tonee and her sister, Sydnee, had been texting back and forth Monday night around the time Tonee left Dobra Tea, but Sydnee didn't hear from her the rest of the night. At the time, she wasn't particularly concerned; she knew that Tonee had to get up early for work and assumed that she would talk to her the following day.

Tonee worked full-time as a metal fabricator at Studebaker Metals, a jewelry shop in Braddock, Pennsylvania. She was scheduled to work at 8:00 am Tuesday morning but failed to show up for her shift. This was completely out of character for Tonee, who was known as a competent and dependable employee; she never missed work without calling her supervisor first. When they learned that Tonee wasn't at work, the fact that her purse had been found on a bridge suddenly seemed much more ominous. They called the Pittsburgh Police Department and reported Tonee missing.

No one can say for certain if Tonee made it back to her house Monday night; her roommate was out of town for the holidays and none of her neighbors recalled seeing her. The red coat she was believed to have been wearing earlier that day was found at her house, however, so it seems likely that she arrived there safely. At some point, she may have gone back out; whether this was voluntary or not remains a mystery.

Hoping to find some clues to her disappearance, her family members paged through Tonee's journal. Although there were some entries where she wrote about feeling sad, she certainly didn't seem despondent and there was nothing to suggest that she might have been considering suicide. Because of where her belongings had been found, however, it was something that couldn't be completely ruled out; friends and family decided to search the area underneath the Homestead Grays Bridge for any indication that Tonee had jumped off of it.

The bridge, which spans the Monongahela River, connects the suburb of Homestead and the city of Pittsburgh. At its highest point, the bridge stands 108 feet above the river; it's possible to survive a fall from this height but unlikely. The Homestead Grays Bridge has been the site of suicides in the past, most recently in June 2019 when a woman parked her car on the bridge and jumped over the side. Several people witnessed her do this, and her body was found in the river two hours later. This seems to always be the case when bodies end up in the Monongahela; if Tonee had jumped, her body should have been recovered. Despite an extensive search by both family and the police, no trace of her was found.

No one who knew Tonee believed that she would

have taken her own life. Sydnee noted, "She was going through the very normal ups and downs of being a young adult, finding her place in the world...she was at a high point."

On Wednesday, 36 hours after Tonee was last seen, the Pittsburgh Police posted a picture of Tonee on their Facebook page and asked for help in locating her. The post was shared 867 times, but failed to help police find the missing woman. On her own Facebook page, Sydnee wrote that the family believed Tonee might be traveling on Interstate 80, though she didn't say why. She noted "We do not trust anyone she is traveling with" and asked for anyone living along the I-80 corridor to be particularly vigilant.

On Thursday, investigators went to Dobra Tea and spoke with employees who had been working on Monday. Marina Fec, the employee who had waited on Tonee that night, told police that the missing woman was a regular customer at the tea shop and had been chatting with another woman when she stopped by on Monday night. "She was pretty quiet, but she's not usually super-talkative." She bought her tea, said goodbye to the employees, and then walked out of the shop.

That Friday, family members received a tip that Tonee had been seen in Pittsburgh's Hill District. This wasn't a part of town that Tonee was known to frequent, but they considered the tip to be credible. Along with a Pittsburgh police officer, the family spent the day going door to door on Linton Street, passing out flyers and asking residents if they had seen the missing woman. Although they had been optimistic about the tip, they found no trace of Tonee. Sydnee noted to a reporter, "There would be nothing here for Tonee."

Tonee was well-known in the Braddock community

and word of her disappearance spread quickly. On Saturday, friends and family held a vigil for Tonee at Braddock's Carnegie Library, where Tonee worked part-time as a ceramics teacher. More than 100 people crowded into the library's art lending room for the vigil, many of them clutching white candles as they prayed for Tonee to come home.

Tonee was described as having a magnetic personality that drew people to her; she was best known for her artwork, her love of music, and the wonderful hugs she gave. Her friend Alexandra Aks noted, "She was able to meet a person and they'd instantly love her."

Tonee's mother attended the vigil; she was grateful to see how many people cared about her daughter but admitted, "I'm starting to fear the worst because of the time that's gone by without hearing anything from her...I don't know how I'm going to go on without her here." Another friend, Malcolm Thomas, stated that he was trying to remain positive about the situation. "Personally, I just refuse to accept that she's not somewhere around."

Tonee was an artist, educator, and dancer who grew up in the Pittsburgh area. She had loved art from an early age and had gotten in trouble with her mother after drawing on the walls when she was little. She was very active with the Braddock Youth Project, first as a participant and then as a leader after she joined AmeriCorps. Shortly after she went missing, the moderator for the Braddock Youth Project Facebook page posted, "So many have grown accustomed to feeling her radiate love amongst different parts of the Braddock community." Like everyone else in the area, they were praying for her safe return.

Sydnee tried to remain optimistic that her sister would be found safe. "Sleeplessness, not eating, anxiety, panic, hope...all throughout there has been this tangible hope and it's getting stronger and stronger every day." She did everything she could to spread the word about Tonee's disappearance, giving several television and radio interviews about the case. As weeks went by, however, the news media appeared to lose interest in the disappearance and Tonee's case faded from the headlines.

Two weeks after Tonee went missing, loved ones held a prayer circle and dance meditation session in her honor. Dozens attended the event, held at the Glitter Box Theater in Pittsburgh. Sydnee, who hosted the event, noted, "The thoughts and prayers are tangible and as a community, they're the most powerful thing that we have to find Tonee."

Nearly a year after Tonee was last seen, her friends and family held a silent march to remember Tonee. All of her loved ones still held out hope that she would be found safe, and they hoped that the march would remind the public that she was still missing. Sydnee told a reporter, "It's just a very sad norm, not having your sister in your life." She wanted the march to commemorate not only Tonee but all missing people.

Although the family was initially satisfied with the Pittsburgh Police Department and their efforts to find Tonee, in a June 2021 interview Sydnee admitted that she was not happy with them. "I feel as though they could have pushed more...I think they really leaned on this idea that she committed suicide." She wondered if the investigation was lax because of the fact that her sister was a black woman.

According to the Pittsburgh Police Department, their investigation into Tonee's disappearance is still active, but little progress has been made in the past two years. Tonee's loved ones know no more now than they did the on night that Tonee's belongings were found, but they continue to hope that Tonee is out there somewhere, safe and happy.

Tonee Turner was 22 years old when she went missing in December 2019. She has a vivacious personality and is an extremely talented artist, and she is very much missed by her Braddock, Pennsylvania, community. Tonee has brown eyes and black hair, and at the time of her disappearance, she was 5 feet 3 inches tall and weighed 130 pounds. Tonee was last seen wearing gray cargo pants, a gray shirt with "Habla Español" written in orange on the back, and a black zip-up jacket. Her ears, nose, and bottom lip are pierced, and she has a spiral tattoo on her left shoulder. If you have any information about Tonee, please contact the Pittsburgh Police Department at 412-323-7800.

Christina Whittaker

Christina Whittaker hadn't had a night out in months, so she was excited to meet up with some friends at a Hannibal, Missouri bar on the evening of Friday, November 13, 2009. It was the first time the 21-year-old had gone out since her daughter had been born six months ago, and she was looking forward to a relaxing night out. Unfortunately, the night didn't go as planned. Christina had a little too much to drink and was kicked out of the bar after she started harassing the bartender, but her friends stayed at the bar, leaving Christina with no way to get home. After trying unsuccessfully to find someone willing to drive her home, Christina vanished. She never made it home and was never seen again.

Christina's boyfriend, Travis Blackwell, had agreed to babysit Christina's daughter, Alexandria, so she could have a night out with her friends. He dropped her off at Rookie's Sports Bar in downtown Hannibal around 8:45 pm; her friends were already at the bar at that time.

Around 10:30 pm, Christina called Travis to check up on her daughter. She assured him that one of her friends would be giving her a ride home around midnight; she also promised to stop at a restaurant and pick up some takeout for him on her way home. It was a promise she wouldn't be able to keep.

By 11:45 pm, Christina had been drinking for three hours. Christina wasn't normally a heavy drinker, but on this night a man at the bar kept buying shots for her and her friends. As a result, she drank more than usual and was very intoxicated. Vicki Lieurance, the bartender at Rookie's Sports Bar, noticed that Christina's behavior changed as she continued to drink. "She was getting belligerent towards me and I told her, 'Well, we're going to ask you to leave.'"

Christina wasn't willing to leave the bar without a fight. Vicki noted, "My boss went over there with me and we both asked her real nice to leave. She wanted to fight, so he grabbed her on one side, I grabbed her on the other side, and we just walked her to the back door."

Curtis Gaines, the bouncer at Rookie's Sports Bar, told reporters that Christina immediately tried to get back in the bar. After he told her that she had to leave, she exited the bar with at least one unidentified male. "I don't remember if there was one or two guys, but one guy came in and grabbed her and then they actually left." Other witnesses claimed she left with as many as four men, but no one seemed to know who they were.

According to Christina's mother, Cindy Young, Christina begged the bouncer and bartender to let her back inside so she could talk to her friends about getting a ride home, but they refused her entry. None of her friends wanted to leave the bar, and they refused to go outside to speak with Christina.

After she was kicked out of Rookie's, Christina went to River City Billiards, which was located right next to Rookies. Once inside, she asked several patrons if they could give her a ride home but none of them were willing to help her out. Eventually, the bartender had enough of Christina pestering customers for a ride and told her she had to leave the bar.

Christina left River City Billiards and wandered around the corner to Sportsman's Bar. The bartender there, Vanessa Swank, had known Christina her entire life.

She said that Christina came into the bar shortly before they closed and mentioned that she had been kicked out of both Rookie's and River City Billiards. "She was on the phone with this guy and they kept arguing back and forth, and finally she just put her phone down and I said, 'Why don't you let me call you a cab and you can go home to your mom's.'"

Christina ignored Vanessa's offer to call a cab. "The next thing I know, she darted out the back door, and that was the last time we all saw her." Witnesses said that Christina was sobbing hysterically when she raced out of the bar; she was alone at the time and there was no indication that anyone had followed her to Sportsman's Bar.

Exactly what happened after Christina left Sportsman's Bar remains unclear, but she never made it home. Travis fell asleep while he was waiting for her to arrive, so he didn't realize anything was wrong until he woke up early Saturday morning. When he was unable to reach Christina on her cell phone, he called her mother, who was out of town for the night. Cindy immediately rushed back to Hannibal.

Although Cindy was certain that Christina wouldn't have voluntarily left her infant daughter, she tried to remain optimistic. She didn't report her missing until the following day, after she learned that someone had found Christina's cell phone early Saturday morning. It had been lying on the sidewalk outside an apartment complex located just yards away from Sportsman's Bar.

Cindy told police that her daughter suffered from several medical conditions that made her especially vulnerable; she had been diagnosed with fibromyalgia, anxiety, bipolar disorder, and depression. She was prescribed several medications that she was supposed to take on a daily basis, but she didn't like the way they made her feel and didn't always take them like she was supposed to. She didn't have any of her prescriptions with her when she disappeared.

According to Cindy, her daughter was somewhat childlike and naïve, and she believed that her psychiatric conditions made her particularly susceptible to manipulation. She worried that Christina had been abducted and might have been a victim of human trafficking.

The Hannibal Police Department used search dogs to try and trace the route Christina had taken when she left Sportsman's Bar. The dogs did appear to pick up on a scent trail but were unable to lead investigators to Christina.

Worried that Christina might have somehow ended up in the Mississippi River, water patrol boats combed the waterway for any sign of her. Like the ground search, the search of the river also came up empty. Hannibal Police Captain James Hark told reporters, "There's nothing to indicate foul play. We're not ruling that out, but we're pursuing all angles at this point."

According to Hannibal Police Lt. Jennifer Grote, "We started contacting the people at the bars where she was at, we checked hotels, we checked hospitals. We did a neighborhood canvas of the area. We extensively interviewed the person who located the phone." They combed through the surrounding area, checking in dumpsters and going door-to-door interviewing residents. Nothing brought them any closer to finding Christina.

Cindy spent the next week prowling the streets of Hannibal, handing out missing person flyers and asking everyone she saw if they had any information about her missing daughter. Any time she got a potential lead, she phoned the Hannibal Police Department and relayed the information to investigators, hoping they would quickly follow up on it.

Rumors about what had happened to Christina soon flooded Hannibal. Some believed that Travis had killed her, either intentionally or accidentally. Others claimed that she had been kidnapped by sex traffickers and forced into prostitution in Peoria, Illinois. Some people thought that she had simply decided to leave Hannibal and start a new life somewhere else. Investigators had to wade through all the rumors but were unable to find any solid evidence pointing to what had happened to Christina.

The most persistent rumor involved a man named Darcy Moore, who was called Bookie on the street. Several different people claimed that he had been the person who kidnapped Christina and was forcing her to work in the sex trade in Peoria. Three weeks after Christina was last seen, investigators interviewed Bookie while he was being held in the Peoria County Jail on unrelated charges. He denied having anything to do with Christina's disappearance and claimed he had been out of town with his wife at the time she went missing. His wife supported his alibi, and detectives were unable to link him to Christina.

In February 2010, Cindy and her husband, Alex, were guests on "The Steve Wilkos Show." They hoped their appearance would bring some much-needed publicity to the case and raise awareness about the fact that Christina was still missing. Christina's boyfriend also appeared on the show, as did Dustin Johnston, the father of Christina's daughter.

Steve Wilkos immediately focused his attention on Travis, directly accusing him of harming Christina and hiding her body. He claimed that Travis had failed two polygraph examinations that had been administered by the show's producers. Travis vehemently denied having anything to do with Christina's disappearance.

Cindy was furious. She stood up for Travis, stating that she was certain he would never harm her daughter. She later told reporters that she was unhappy with the way the show handled the situation. "I am so disappointed in them. We went on the show to get help to find Christy and all they did was make Travis look like a monster...I was so upset."

Cindy noted that it would have been impossible for Travis to have done anything to Christina as he was at the house with Alexandria the entire time. "I know he would never do anything to hurt her. He was here that night...my son and his girlfriend were right across the hall." They confirmed that Travis had never left the house.

Hoping to set the story straight, Travis went to the Hannibal police and voluntarily submitted to a polygraph examination there. He passed. It didn't stop all the rumors circulating about his possible involvement, but investigators didn't consider him a suspect.

Disappointed with the way the Hannibal Police Department was handling the case, Cindy started working with a private investigator. In March 2011, the private detective told reporters that he believed Christina was alive and being held against her will in Peoria. He claimed there had been several reports of sightings there, but police said that none of these sightings could be confirmed.

Peoria police officer Doug Burgess told reporters, "We've spoken with the family, who has given us information that they've spoken with people who have seen her in the area, but we have absolutely no confirmed accounts that she's in this area." He did admit that several members of the Peoria Police Department's narcotics unit believed they had seen Christina in February 2010 but she had raced off as soon as she saw them. "There's absolutely no way to confirm whether it was her or not, but they did say that the picture [of Christina] looked like the girl who ran from them."

In May 2011, Cindy told reporters that the pain of missing Christina remained as strong as it had been when she first vanished. "When you have a nightmare, you wake up from it. We don't get to wake up. My daughter is gone...I've been told she's dead many times. I don't believe that. God put it in my heart she's alive, and I know she'll come home."

Christina's case eventually faded from the headlines and the investigation into her disappearance started to go cold. Cindy did everything she could to keep the case in the public eye, and she continued to receive reports of potential sightings of Christina. Almost all of these sightings were in Peoria, and Cindy was convinced that Christina was still alive and being forced to work as a prostitute there by her abductors. "My daughter's a very pretty girl. They saw her and knew they could make money off her and that's exactly what they did."

According to Hannibal Police Lt. John Zerbonia, "We have been to Peoria on several different occasions. We've checked stores, residences, and gas stations. We even sent officers undercover to Peoria bars and strip clubs to see if they had any evidence that what we were hearing was true." They weren't able to confirm any of the rumors about Christina being in the Peoria area.

Christina's loved ones held prayer vigils and balloon releases each year on the anniversary of the disappearance. By 2017, she had been missing for eight years but her family still believed that she was alive and would one day be returned to them. Alexandria, who had celebrated her 8th birthday without her mother, spoke at the 2017 vigil and told reporters, "I miss her and I love her and I want her to come home." She was living in Palmyra with her father, but continued to think about her mother daily. She admitted that the top request on her Christmas list each year was for her mother to come home.

In September 2018, police received a tip that Christina's body was buried on a property in Marion County, Missouri. According to Lt. Jennifer Grote, investigators thought it was a credible lead. "We contacted the FBI, and they brought their dig team up. They dug in the area that we were given information on and we have no findings from that." It was simply one more rumor.

As the 10th anniversary of Christina's disappearance approached, Hannibal detectives said they were still trying to determine what had happened to her. Hannibal Police Chief Lyndell Davis admitted, "We know that in the public's mind a case like this might be forgotten by some or never even heard of by others. We thought it might be time to ignite some new interest in the case...this is still an open investigation."

Lt. Jennifer Grote, who had been working the case since the beginning, said the case was tough because they heard so many different rumors about Christina's fate but had no solid evidence to back any of them up. "We've talked to over 200 people...we've gone coast to coast following leads and tips on this case." Despite the extensive investigation, detectives still have no idea what happened to Christina but believe there are people out there who do know. They continue to hope that someone will call them with the information they need to finally close this case.

Christina Maxine Whittaker was just 21 years old when she went missing in Hannibal, Missouri in November 2009. There are dozens of rumors about what happened to her, but no solid evidence and police have no idea if she is alive or dead. Christina has brown eyes and red hair, and at the time of her disappearance, she was 5 feet 5 inches tall and weighed 125 pounds. She has a scar from a Cesarean section on her abdomen and a surgical scar on her left knee. She has a tattoo of an angel on her back and one of a Care Bear on her ankle. She was last seen wearing a pink tank top under a white V-neck shirt, blue jeans, and white Nike sneakers with pink stripes. If you have any information about Christina, please contact the Hannibal Police Department at 573-221-0987.

Sydney West

Sydney West got up early on the morning of Wednesday, September 30, 2020, and left the San Francisco home where she was staying with friends. The 19-year-old used a rideshare service to get to the Golden Gate Bridge, a place she went often to take pictures and exercise. At 6:45 am, she started making her way across the bridge in the direction of Crissy Field, but she never made it off the bridge. At some point during her walk, Sydney vanished without a trace.

Sydney – known as Syd to friends and family – had grown up in Pleasanton, California, but had moved to Chapel Hill, North Carolina, when she was in high school. A 2019 graduate of Carrboro High School, she decided to take a gap year when she didn't get into her first choice college. She spent her gap year traveling in Australia and spending time with her family. She seemed to struggle with a little bit of depression as she watched her friends start college but her mood brightened when she learned that she had been accepted into the University of California at Berkeley for the fall of 2020.

Syd had suffered a concussion during the summer of 2020, and she hadn't fully recovered by the time she moved to California in August 2020. Her father, Jay West, later stated that dropping her off at Berkeley had been hard for both Syd and her parents. She experienced some anxiety about being so far away from her parents, sister, and dog, but was looking forward to going back to school.

Although Syd had initially been very excited about

starting her freshman year, the COVID-19 pandemic meant that all of her classes were held online, with little in-person interaction. Feeling isolated and still suffering from the effects of the concussion, Syd made the difficult decision to withdraw from her classes and defer her enrollment for a year.

Syd moved out of her college dormitory but decided that she wanted to remain in California for a while, so she went to stay with some family friends who lived in the Bay area. She remained extremely close with her parents and younger sister in North Carolina and was in constant phone contact with them. She last spoke to her father on September 29th; they had an hour-long phone conversation and made plans to speak again the following day.

Jay knew something was wrong when he was unable to reach his daughter the following day. After repeated calls to her cell phone went unanswered, he used an app to try and locate her phone. It appeared that her phone had been turned off, however, and Jay was unable to determine its location. He called the friends Syd was staying with and learned that they hadn't seen Syd at all that day. Concerned, he told his wife, Kimberly, that he couldn't get a hold of their daughter and he was worried about her.

Syd's parents went online and checked her bank account to see if they could glean any information from it, but it showed no recent activity. When there was still no word from Syd by the next morning, Jay and Kimberly knew that something was terribly wrong. They called police and reported their daughter missing.

Since Syd was a permanent resident of North Carolina, she had to be reported missing to police there. Officials in North Carolina then contacted police in San

Francisco, where Syd had been living. Through their investigation, they learned that Syd had been dropped off by a rideshare driver near the Golden Gate Bridge Wednesday morning, but her trail appeared to end there.

The driver was interviewed extensively but wasn't able to provide investigators with much information. He had simply dropped Syd off and then went on his way. If he had any observations about her mood or behavior that morning, they were not released to the public. Detectives did state that the driver had been cooperative in the investigation and was not considered a suspect in Syd's disappearance.

There are numerous cameras on the Golden Gate Bridge and one of them captured Syd as she started to make her way across. Unfortunately, it was an extremely foggy morning and she soon disappeared from view. Much of the bridge was completely obscured by fog, making it impossible for investigators to determine what happened to Syd after she vanished into the mist.

When asked what he thought might have happened to his daughter, Jay stated, "The reality is, I'm her father, I saw the video on the bridge, and I don't know." There was no evidence indicating that she jumped off the bridge and nothing pointing towards an abduction. Syd had simply vanished without leaving any clues as to what had happened to her.

Sydney had spent most of her life in Pleasanton, California. She was a talented singer and songwriter who had showcased her musical prowess at many open mic nights. She went to Foothill High School in Pleasanton for her freshman and sophomore years; she was very athletic and played on the school's volleyball team.

The move to North Carolina meant that Syd had to switch schools at the start of her junior year, but it didn't seem to bother her too much. She was quickly accepted by classmates at Carrboro High School and became the co-captain of the volleyball team at her new school. In her personal statement on the NCAA sports website, Syd noted, "Volleyball has taught me to never underestimate my skills and the importance of being a leader...through sheer will and hard work, I can accomplish whatever goals I set."

One of Syd's goals had been to go to UC Berkeley, and she had been thrilled when she learned it was going to be a reality. Yet even though she had accomplished her college goal, Syd still struggled with some mental health issues. In a televised interview, her father stated, "She is a wonderful human being...she's also a human being that struggled with anxiety and depression and it got a hold of her. He noted that she had been sad in their final conversation, but had told him that she loved him and said she would talk to him the next day. He had no idea it would be the last time he would speak to her.

It's unclear what Syd's intentions were when she started her trek across the Golden Gate Bridge that morning, but she would make the one-mile walk across it to exercise in Crissy Field. It's very possible that was what she planned on doing that morning; it's also possible that her depression had finally overtaken her and she intended to end her life. It is the complete lack of evidence that bothers her family.

Her mother, Kimberly, noted that there were dozens of other people on the bridge at the same time as Syd that morning. "There were people walking, running, biking, driving...the fact that all of our pleas to the public and all of the information out there but nobody has seen anything is just so baffling to us."

When Syd arrived at the Golden Gate Bridge, she

was wearing a pair of dark-colored leggings, a teal hooded sweatshirt, and a pair of Vans sneakers with palm trees on them. Her hair was in a bun and she was carrying a small backpack; it looked as if she were ready for an early-morning exercise session. Her backpack was later found on the bridge and turned over to police; her cell phone was never recovered.

All of Syd's social media accounts went silent after September 30th. There was no further activity on her cell phone or her bank account, and she left most of her belongings, including all of her clothing and her laptop, at the home where she was staying. She didn't leave any kind of note behind and there was nothing found in her belongings to suggest that she intended on harming herself.

Both investigators and Syd's family made public appeals for information, but if anyone had seen Syd on the bridge that morning they didn't come forward. Three weeks after she was seen, a vigil was held for Syd in Pleasanton's Lions Wayside Park. Childhood friends were among those who gathered to show their support for Syd, all of them praying that she would be found.

Although the San Francisco Police Department received a few tips regarding Syd's possible location, none of them panned out. A month after Syd was last seen, a spokesperson for the police department had little to say about the investigation, noting only that Sydney was still classified as a missing person and the investigation was ongoing.

Desperate to find their daughter, Jay and Kimberly announced that they were offering a $10,000 reward for information leading to Syd's location or to the person responsible for her disappearance. Investigators received a few tips, but no substantial leads were developed and the reward money went unclaimed.

As of December 2023, Syd's disappearance remains unsolved and investigators don't know anything more than they did on the day she vanished. Due to the fact that she was known to be depressed, she is classified as an "at-risk" missing person. Her family remains committed to finding her and bringing her home; the reward for information is currently up to $25,000.

Sydney West was 19 years old when she went missing in 2020. She was passionate about animals, the environment, music, and volleyball and had been looking forward to attending her dream college until the COVID-19 pandemic occurred. Although she was no longer in school at the time of her disappearance, she was planning to return to classes in the fall of 2021. Syd has dark blonde hair and blue eyes; she is 5 feet 10 inches tall and weighs 135 pounds. She was last seen wearing a light teal hooded sweatshirt, black leggings, and black Vans sneakers with palm trees on them. Although she usually wore contacts, she is believed to have been wearing her glasses when she disappeared. If you have any information about Sydney, please contact the San Francisco Police Department at 415-553-0123.

Printed in Great Britain
by Amazon

35345646R00106